Editor
Andrea Tropeano, M.A.

Cover Artist
Brenda DiAntonis

Editor in Chief
Ina Massler Levin, M.A.

Creative Director
Karen J. Goldfluss, M.S. Ed.

Art Coordinator
Renée Christine Yates

Imaging
Leonard P. Swierski

Publisher
Mary D. Smith, M.S. Ed.

Teacher Created Resources
TCR 2896

MW00636784

Prepare & [...] for [...]
STANDARDIZED TESTS
Grade 6

LANGUAGE ARTS

MATH

SOCIAL STUDIES

SCIENCE

Includes Standards

Includes a variety of strategies for successful test taking

Offers helpful tips and suggestions to reduce test anxiety

Teacher Created Resources

Author
Julia McMeans, M.Ed.

Teacher Created Resources, Inc.
6421 Industry Way
Westminster, CA 92683
www.teachercreated.com

ISBN: 978-1-4206-2896-8

©2009 Teacher Created Resources, Inc.
Reprinted, 2012
Made in U.S.A.

Teacher Created Resources

Table of Contents

Introduction

Standardized tests have not only been the subject of intense controversy among educators, but also the cause of much teeth gnashing among students. If individuals are unique, and learning styles and ways of understanding vary, how then can a standardized test accurately measure what a student knows?

There is a story of a first-grade teacher who held up a red apple to her class of 30 eager students and asked, "What color is this apple?" Twenty-nine of the students replied, "It's red," while one brave soul countered, "It's red and white." "Oh," the teacher responded, "I don't see any white," to which the student replied, "That's because you have to bite it!"

This is a cautionary tale that demonstrates that there are multiple ways in which to know, and that they can all potentially be correct. For this reason, it is critical that both educators and students understand what standardized tests seek to measure and the best strategies to prepare for and take these kinds of tests.

The vast majority of standardized tests that students encounter during their academic careers, including the California Achievement Test, the Iowa Test, and the Stanford Achievement Test, are norm-referenced tests. Norm-referenced tests compare and rank students in a particular grade with other students in that same grade. By doing this, educators can get a quick snapshot of where their students stand and to what extent their scores deviate from the average or the norm.

The content contained on standardized tests is aligned with statewide curriculum standards, and vice versa. If a skill set appears in your content standards, it is reasonable to expect that it may appear on a standardized test. For example, you will never find a problem such as this on a fourth-grade standardized test:

$(4x - 2x^2 - 7xy) + (2x^2 + 5xy)$

However, you would very likely find a problem like this: 63 x 59.

The reason is clear—the addition and subtraction of polynomials is not part of the fourth-grade core content for math, while the multiplication of two-digit numbers is.

It is imperative that students understand how standardized tests are scored, what they measure, and the kind of material they will encounter. By sharing this behind-the-scenes aspect of standardized tests with your students, you will help to empower them by demystifying the tests themselves, and thus reducing the high anxiety often associated with them.

Standardized tests can be an effective measurement tool. Over the years, great steps have been taken not only to improve standardized testing—for instance, paying particular attention to bias in order to create tests that are more equitable—but also to provide students with an array of strategies that they can use in test-taking situations.

The purpose of this book is to help educators and students prepare for standardized tests by providing general information on test-taking strategies, tips on stress and anxiety reduction, and a variety of practice tests that span the core content that appears on these types of tests.

The practice tests contained within this book are arranged according to content area and then to specific skill sets within that area. The test questions are written in the style most frequently used on standardized tests and are aligned with the McRel Compendium of Content Standards. Blank student answer sheets are provided on page 135.

McRel Compendium of Content Standards and Skills Index

Content Area	Standards Covered	Specific Skills Covered
Writing	• Uses the general skills and strategies of the writing process. • Uses the stylistic and rhetorical aspects of writing. • Uses grammatical and mechanical conventions in written compositions. • Gathers and uses information for research purposes.	Capitalization • Combining • Conjugation • Contractions • Editing • Elaborating • Paragraphing • Pronoun Referents • Punctuation • Spelling • Subject-Verb Agreement • Types of Sentences • Usage
Reading	• Uses the general skills and strategies of the reading process. • Uses reading skills and strategies to understand and interpret a variety of literary texts. • Uses reading skills and strategies to understand and interpret a variety of informational texts.	**Reading Comprehension:** Author's Purpose • Cause and Effect • Compare and Contrast • Conflict • Fact versus Opinion • Fiction • Figurative Language • Inferences • Main Idea • Nonfiction • Plot • Poetry • Point of View • Prediction • Literary Genres • Research • Rhyming • Sequencing • Setting • Supporting Details • Topic Sentence **Vocabulary:** Affixes • Antonyms • Homographs • Syllabication • Synonyms
Math	• Uses a variety of strategies in the problem solving process. • Understands and applies basic and advanced properties of the concepts of numbers. • Uses basic and advanced procedures while performing the processes of computation. • Understands and applies basic and advanced properties of the concepts of measurement. • Understands and applies basic and advanced properties of the concepts of geometry. • Understands and applies basic and advanced properties of the concepts of statistics and data analysis. • Understands and applies basic and advanced properties of the concepts of probability. • Understands and applies basic and advanced properties of functions and algebra. • Understands the general nature and uses of mathematics.	**Number Concepts:** Prime and Composite Numbers • Factors and Multiples • Odd and Even Numbers • Equivalency of Basic Percents, Fractions, and Decimals • Place Value • Ordering and Comparing Whole Numbers, Fractions, and Decimals • Greater Numbers **Computation:** Addition and Subtraction of Whole Numbers • Multiplication and Division of Whole Numbers • Addition and Subtraction of Simple Fractions with Like and Unlike Denominators • Mixed Numbers and Improper Fractions • Simplest Form • Addition and Subtraction of Decimals • Rounding • Money **Measurement:** Perimeter • Area • Volume • Capacity • Mass • Angle • Circumference • Standard Units • Time **Geometry:** Solids • Plane Figures • Properties of Figures • Congruent or Similar • Transformations • Lines, Rays, Segments, and Angles **Statistics and Data Analysis:** Mean, Median, and Mode • Graphs, Plots, and Charts **Probability:** Outcomes and Predictions **Algebra:** Patterns and Rules • Variables • Equations • Expressions • Open Sentences • Coordinate System • Word Problems

McRel Compendium of Content Standards and Skills Index

Content Area	Standards Covered	Specific Skills Covered
Science	• Understands atmospheric processes and the water cycle. • Understands Earth's composition and structure. • Understands the composition and structure of the universe. • Understands the principles of heredity and related concepts. • Understands the structure and function of cells and organisms. • Understands the relationship among organisms and their physical environments. • Understands biological evolution and the diversity of life. • Understands the structure and properties of matter. • Understands the sources and properties of energy. • Understands forces and motion. • Understands the nature of scientific inquiry. • Understands the scientific enterprise.	Animals • Earth • Ecosystems • Electricity and Magnetism • Human Body • Matter • Oceans • Plants • Solar System • Weather
Geography	• The World in Spatial Terms • Places and Regions • Physical Systems • Human Systems • Environment and Society • Uses of Geography	Maps • Globes
History	• Living and Working Together in Families and Communities, Now and Long Ago • The History of the United States: Democratic Principles and Values and the People from Many Cultures who Contributed to its Cultural, Economic, and Political Heritage • The History of Peoples of Many Cultures Around the World	Citizenship • Government

General Test-Taking Strategies

A student's performance on a standardized test is influenced by many things—some are obvious, while others are elusive. Also, there are many factors over which educators have control, while there are many others over which they do not. Until someone invents a magic wand, word, or potion that can be waved over, said to, or imbibed by students, educators will have to rely on more conventional methods to help their students succeed on standardized tests. Below is a list of some general test-taking guidelines with which students should be familiar.

1. Get a good night's sleep the night before the test. Most people need about eight hours.
2. Avoid caffeinated or sugary drinks before taking the test, as they can make you jittery.
3. Eat a well-balanced meal.
4. Wear comfortable clothing.
5. Read or listen to the directions carefully. If something is unclear, ask for clarification.
6. Wear a watch and budget your time.
7. Find out the rules of the test. Will you be penalized for answering something incorrectly? For leaving something blank? Will partial credit be given?
8. If you get stuck on a question, mark it and move on. You can come back to it later.
9. If the test permits, do a memory check. Jot down important formulas or information on a piece of scrap paper.
10. Use mnemonic devices to jog your memory, such as "never eat soggy waffles" to remember the four compass points: north, east, south, and west.

Reducing Test Anxiety

Anxiety can be debilitating in a test-taking situation, but it is important to remember that not all students experience test anxiety. There is a story about a first-year teacher who entered his room on test day and said jokingly to his seventh-grade class, "Well, is everybody nervous?" A student raised his hand and replied, "I'm nervous that I'm not nervous!"

Some students experience test anxiety, while others do not. And there are students for whom tests occasion a modicum of anxiety that not only does not inhibit their performance, but actually enhances it! The type of test anxiety we are concerned with here is the kind that severely impedes a student's ability to perform on a standardized test. But how do you know when a student has this kind of anxiety? There are several things that might tip you off:

- Tardiness on test day
- Absenteeism on test day
- Crying
- Hyperactivity
- Lethargy
- Jitteriness

- Shallow breathing
- Sweating
- Distractibility/inability to focus/going blank
- Nausea
- Muscle tension

Of course, one of the biggest clues of test anxiety is when a student who demonstrates knowledge and understanding of content via his/her daily classroom performance falls apart when confronted with a standardized test which is assessing the same skills.

Fortunately, there are a variety of strategies that can be taught to students suffering from test anxiety that can help them manage it. These strategies, however, should be routinely practiced by students in order for them to be effective. There is very little point in modeling positive self-talk five minutes before a test and then expecting that it will be of any use.

A Note to the Test Givers

Students are not the only people who experience test anxiety. Teachers, administrators, and other school personnel responsible for administering standardized tests can also experience anxiety around test time as pressure to increase student achievement mounts. While this is understandable, it is important to remember that anxiety is contagious: Anxious educators can often, inadvertently, create anxious students. Be mindful of your demeanor when administering the test. Create a relaxed, positive environment. Smile and maintain your sense of humor. Know that you have done your best to prepare your students. And your best is all you and they can do!

Strategies for Reducing Test Anxiety

The following pages contain some of the most effective strategies available to help elementary, middle, high school, and even college students overcome test anxiety. By familiarizing students with all of these strategies, and providing opportunities for them to practice, students will be better able to determine not only which strategies they are most comfortable using, but which strategies have the greatest impact on reducing their test anxiety.

Positive Self-Talk

Anxiety and negativity are akin to the old chicken-and-egg situation: Does our anxiety cause us to make negative statements to ourselves or do our negative self-statements create the anxiety? Let's just say that test anxiety and negative self-talk are inextricably linked—if you find an anxious student, you will probably also find a student who is telling him/herself that he/she is going to fail. Positive self-talk consists of simple positive, yet realistic, statements and repeating these statements to oneself in an anxiety-provoking situation. Some examples of positive self-talk are:

- ➤ I can do this.
- ➤ I know this material.
- ➤ I have practiced this material.
- ➤ I'm intelligent.

The trick to using this strategy is for students to keep the statements simple and to have them practice using them prior to any test-taking situation. You don't want them to have to come up with the statements at the moment they are confronted with the test!

Visualization

There are essentially two types of creative visualization that can be used to help combat test anxiety. Let us call the first type the *Safe Place Method*, which requires students to conjure a mental image of a place, either real or imagined, that is both relaxing and safe. Provide students with the following instructions in order to practice this method:

- ➤ Close your eyes.
- ➤ Calm your breath.
- ➤ Picture your safe place.
- ➤ Look up and down and to the left and to the right of your safe place.
- ➤ Take notice of what you see, smell, and feel.
- ➤ Smile.

The second visualization technique we will call the *Olympic Method*. This method, often used by athletes, requires that individuals imagine what they are trying to achieve, whether it be crossing the finish line first, hitting a home run, or acing a test! Have students practice the following steps:

- ➤ Close your eyes.
- ➤ Calm your breath.
- ➤ Picture yourself confidently taking the test.
- ➤ Remember another test in which you did well.
- ➤ Imagine yourself receiving a high test score or grade.
- ➤ Smile.

Strategies for Reducing Test Anxiety *(cont.)*

Progressive Muscle Relaxation

Anxiety has both a psychological and physiological component. Muscle tension is a common response to test anxiety that can be minimized by using progressive muscle relaxation. This method involves focusing on and then tensing and relaxing large muscle groups in a particular order.

> ➤ Begin at your toes. Tighten or clench your toes and hold for three to five seconds. Release.
> ➤ Move upward to your feet, calves, thighs, and so forth. Tighten each muscle group for five seconds, then release.
> ➤ Once you have moved through your body, take a few deep breaths.

Controlled Breathing

It is a rare person indeed who has never experienced shallow breathing when in an anxiety-filled situation. In fact, shallow, short breaths are a universal indicator of someone who is overwhelmed by anxiety. Practicing controlled breathing is a simple, yet powerful, way in which to deal with all kinds of anxiety.

> ➤ Sit comfortably.
> ➤ Place your hand on your stomach.
> ➤ Breathe gently in through your nose for a count of four.
> ➤ Let your breath expand your belly. Observe your stomach rising.
> ➤ Breathe out for a count of four. Observe your stomach flattening.
> ➤ Repeat.

No doubt you will have noticed that all of the aforementioned techniques have to do with changing what we say, what we see, and what we feel. The mind and the body are woven tightly together like a carpet, and often all one needs to do to unravel the pattern of test anxiety woven into the fabric is to pull on one tiny thread. In order for these strategies to be successful, however, students must routinely practice them, especially in non-test-taking situations.

Familiarity and proficiency with these methods will empower students and give them the extra tools they need to do their best.

Multiple-Choice Questions

Whether your school or district administers the Iowa Test of Basic Skills, the Terra Nova Achievement Test, or the Texas Assessment of Knowledge and Skills, the vast majority of test questions that students will encounter will be in a multiple-choice format. For this reason, it's important for students to understand not only how these types of questions are constructed and what they are trying to assess, but also what general strategies they can apply to help them arrive at the correct answers.

All multiple-choice questions contain a stem, or incomplete statement, and four to five choices. Only one of the choices is the correct answer, and the others are called decoys, or distractors. The purpose of a multiple-choice question is to determine whether students can tease out the correct information when it is surrounded by incorrect information. For example:

The Declaration of Independence was written by (*stem*)

   Ⓐ **Jefferson Davis.**   (*distractor*)

   Ⓑ **Thomas Jefferson.**   (*correct option*)

   Ⓒ **Jefferson Airplane.**   (*distractor*)

   Ⓓ **George Jefferson.**   (*distractor*)

   Ⓔ **all of the above.**   (*distractor*)

Extreme Words and Statements

Extreme words and statements, like extreme sports, can be dangerous . . . especially on standardized tests. Take, if you will, this rather extreme statement:

I always eat healthy foods.

Ah, if only it were true! The fact is that the word *always* makes this statement extreme and, therefore, very likely to be false. It's not only important for students to understand how words can affect the veracity of statements, but also how to recognize and navigate qualifiers and absolutes in both stems and options.

Absolutes are words such as *always, never, all, none,* and *only.* Words like these tend to make statements false. Because multiple-choice questions often require students to create true statements, by combining stems and options, absolute words, when encountered on standardized tests, should ring the alarm. There are very few things in life for which there are no exceptions. Absolute words close all doors and windows. They do not allow for the possibility of something occurring even once.

Qualifiers are words such as *many, often, some, rarely,* and *may.* These kinds of words tend to make statements true, and when they appear in options could indicate the correct answer. Unlike absolutes, qualifiers leave the door ajar and the window slightly cracked. They allow for the possibility of something occurring even if it only happens once in a blue moon. Try this one with your class:

The class of animals known as mammals

  Ⓐ **never lay eggs.**   *(absolute)*

  Ⓑ **always lay eggs.**   *(absolute)*

  Ⓒ **rarely lay eggs.**   *(qualifier)*

  Ⓓ **None of the above**

Here we have two options in which there are absolute words and one in which there is a qualifier. Now let's try to create some true statements.

  a. It is true that the class of animals known as mammals never lay eggs.

  b. It is true that the class of animals known as mammals always lay eggs.

  c. It is true that the class of animals known as mammals rarely lay eggs.

In order for either *a* or *b* to be correct, it would mean that either there are no mammals, anywhere on the face of the earth, that lay eggs or that all mammals, without exception, lay eggs. Both of these options are extreme and, therefore, likely to be false. While most mammals give birth to live young, there are a few who do indeed lay eggs, such as the duck-billed platypus and the echidna.

Meta Multiple-Choice

Following are several strategies that students can use when confronted by multiple-choice questions and a practice multiple-choice test. The purpose of this test is not to assess content knowledge, but to provide students with an opportunity to both ponder and practice applying these strategies. Copy and distribute pages 13 through 15. Students can work individually, in pairs, or in a larger group. Encourage students to identify which strategies they used and what clues contained within the stems or the options helped them to arrive at the correct answers. Before students begin, it will be important to remind them that these strategies are guidelines and should not be applied thoughtlessly.

The Secrets to Acing Tests!

When we teach our students test-taking strategies, we run the risk of inadvertently implying that it is possible to do well on a test by simply strategizing alone. This, of course, is not the case. No test-taking strategy can take the place of simply knowing the material, and it is important that this be stated explicitly to students. Students who understand the material and who are confident usually don't need strategies to help them do well on tests; and if they do, it is only on about ten percent of the test items. It is critical that students understand that the most important and fool-proof test-taking strategy is simply knowing the material.

Multiple-Choice Strategies

Multiple-choice questions are specifically designed to stump, or trick, the test taker. The following strategies will help you when confronted with all multiple-choice questions.

1. Read the stem carefully.

2. Cover the options and make a prediction.

3. If your prediction or something close to it appears, select it.

4. If your prediction does not appear, read each option carefully.

5. Eliminate any silly options.

6. Eliminate any options you know to be incorrect.

7. A stem and option that creates a grammatically incorrect statement may be an indication that it is wrong.

8. Preface the stem and option choice with the phrase "It is true that. . ." If the stem and option creates a true statement, it is an indication that it is correct.

9. If "All of the above" is an option and at least two of the other options are correct, then select "All of the above."

10. If "All of the above" is an option and you know that at least one of the options is wrong, then eliminate both "All of the above" and the other incorrect option.

11. If "None of the above" is an option and at least one of the options is correct, then eliminate "None of the above" as a possibility.

Multiple-Choice Practice Questions

Directions: Using the strategies you have learned so far, fill in the answer circles for your choices. After you have answered each question, write down which strategy you used and explain why you used it.

1. Lewis and Clark were
   - Ⓐ a famous comedy team.
   - Ⓑ American explorers.
   - Ⓒ English explorers.
   - Ⓓ generals during the American Revolution.

   THINK! Which strategy did you use and why?

2. A word of opposite meaning is
   - Ⓔ a synonym.
   - Ⓕ a homonym.
   - Ⓖ an antonym.
   - Ⓗ a metaphor.

   THINK! Which strategy did you use and why?

3. Which is a region of the United States?
   - Ⓐ Northeast
   - Ⓑ Southeast
   - Ⓒ Midwest
   - Ⓓ West
   - Ⓔ All of the above

   THINK! Which strategy did you use and why?

4. The term *author's point of view* refers to
   - Ⓕ what the author is looking at when he/she writes the story.
   - Ⓖ the author's opinion.
   - Ⓗ the title of the story.
   - Ⓘ the characters in the story.

   THINK! Which strategy did you use and why?

Multiple-Choice Practice Questions *(cont.)*

5. A polygon is
   - (A) a line segment.
   - (B) a sphere.
   - (C) another name for a square.
   - (D) a closed plane figure composed of straight lines.

   THINK! Which strategy did you use and why?

6. The phrase "an apple a day keeps the doctor away" most likely means that
   - (E) doctors are afraid of apples.
   - (F) eating healthy foods helps keep you healthy.
   - (G) doctors refuse to treat patients who eat apples.
   - (H) if you eat apples you will never get sick.

   THINK! Which strategy did you use and why?

7. The shell of an oyster or clam can also be called
   - (A) skin.
   - (B) an exoskeleton.
   - (C) a membrane.
   - (D) a vertebra.

   THINK! Which strategy did you use and why?

8. A quotient is produced by
   - (E) multiplying the factors.
   - (F) adding the addends.
   - (G) dividing the dividend by the divisor.
   - (H) subtracting the numerators.
   - (I) None of the above

   THINK! Which strategy did you use and why?

More Multiple-Choice Practice!

Now that students have some familiarity with the ins and outs of multiple-choice questions, have them participate in the activity described below.

Test Takers to Test Makers!

Students are frequently cast in the role as test takers, but how often do they get to be the test makers? To help students internalize the multiple-choice strategies they have learned, have them participate in the following activity:

- Either in pairs or individually, have students select a content area with which they feel comfortable.
- Ask them to create ten multiple-choice questions based on current classroom learning.
- Tell them that each question must contain a stem and four to five options.
- The options must contain one correct answer and several distractors.
- The distractors should include some of the errors previously discussed.
- When tests are completed, have students swap with each other to not only take the test, but to also practice using the various multiple-choice strategies and identifying various types of errors.

Getting to Know Test Structure

While the element of surprise is great when it comes to a pun, plot, or party, it can be the proverbial kiss of death when it comes to a standardized test! Standardized tests come in particular forms, and just as it is important for students to know the content they may encounter and the strategies that they can use, they will also need to become familiar with the physicality of the test itself. In other words, they should be familiar with how the test is organized, how to mark their answers, and when and where to stop throughout the test. To increase the odds of students doing their best, make sure that they understand the following:

Remember. . .

- Standardized tests are given to thousands of students and are marked or graded by a computer. The computer will not interpret your answer the way your teacher might. It will either mark an answer right or wrong.
- Fill in each bubble completely and stay within the lines.
- If you need to erase, do so completely.
- Do not make any stray marks on the test sheet. Use scrap paper to work out problems or jot down ideas.
- Make sure that the answer you mark corresponds to the question being asked.
- Look for the words STOP and GO in the lower right-hand corner of test pages. These words will indicate whether or not you are finished or if there are more pages to complete.

Marking Your Answers

The purpose of this lesson is to introduce you to the correct way to mark your answers on a standardized test.

A standardized test is one that is given to thousands and thousands of students. The writers of the questions try to be as fair as possible. After all, it wouldn't mean anything if all sixth-grade students took different kinds of tests—some easy, some hard. The results would be confusing and meaningless.

The scoring of standardized tests tries to be as fair as possible, too. It is done by a computer. However, for computer-scored tests, answer sheets must be marked the same way by all students. This is why everyone must use a pencil marked No. 2 and fill in the circles with dark marks.

Attention must also be paid to how a question is written. For example, a question on a standardized test might look like this:

Directions: Fill in the answer circle for your choice.

How do you write the plural of the word *mouse*?

      mouses   mices   mice   meeses

       ○   ○   ○   ○

You would fill in the circle below *mice*. But what if the question were written this way?

Directions: Fill in the answer circle for your choice.

How do you write the plural of *house*?
- Ⓐ hice
- Ⓑ hices
- Ⓒ hoose
- Ⓓ houses

You would fill in the circle with D inside of it, not fill in the (D) before the word *houses*. If you did that, the computer would mark your answer as incorrect. Unfortunately, the computer would have no way of determining that you knew the plural of house!

Marking Your Answers *(cont.)*

Of course, you will not fill in answers as soon as you are handed a standardized test. The first thing you will do is put your name on the answer sheet. Here is an example:

Each filled-in circle stands for a letter in someone's name. Figure out the person's name by looking at the filled-in circles and then writing the letter of the circle in the empty box above the row. Notice that the person filled in blank circles for spaces anywhere in her name, including leftover spaces at the end. Circles must be filled in under every box.

Did you figure out the person's name?

| Last Name | | | | | | | | | | | | | | | First Name | | | | | | | | | | | |

(Bubble grid with columns A–Z for Last Name and First Name, selected circles filling in the name.)

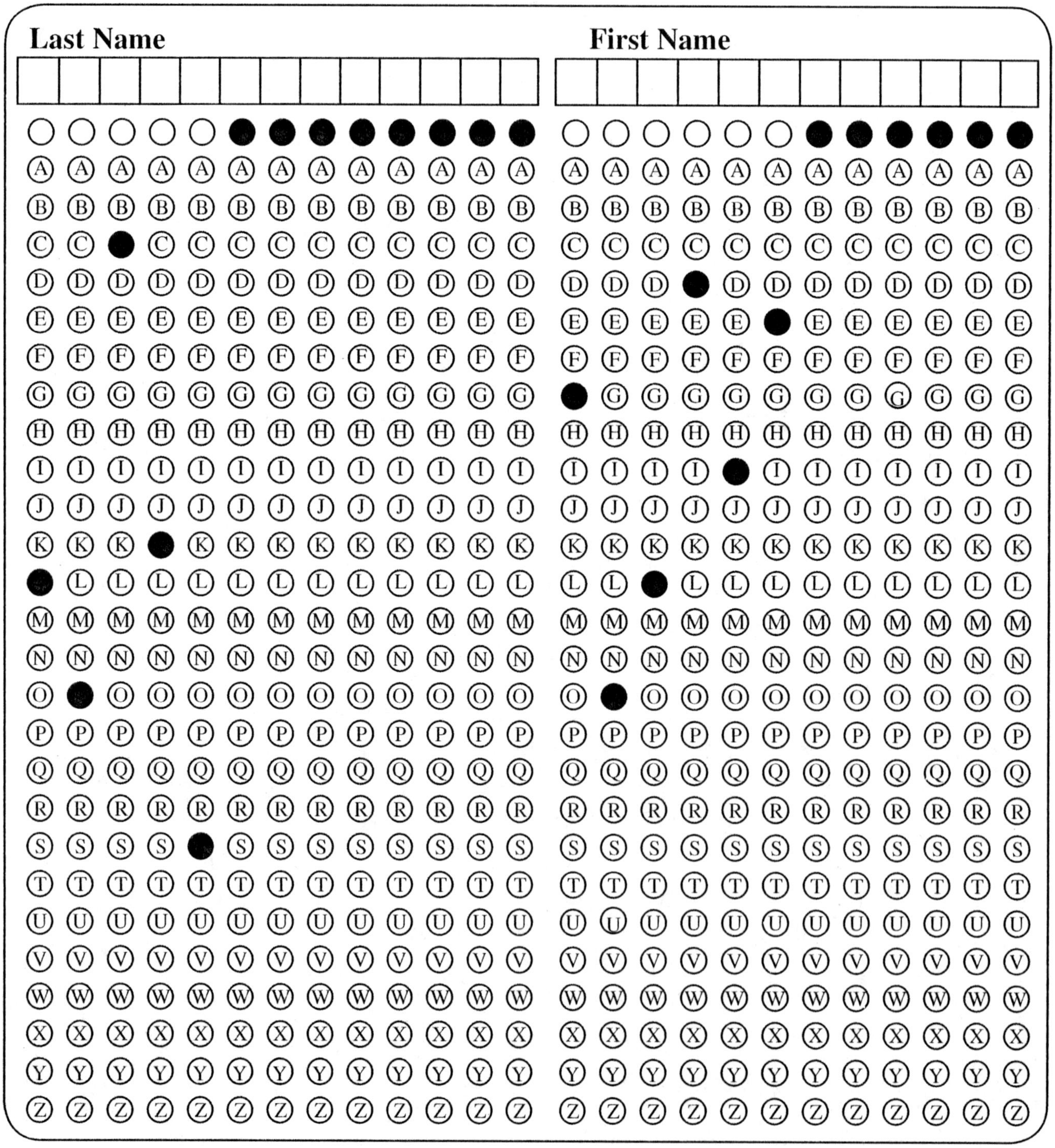

Literal, Inferential, and Analytical Questions

Standardized tests will always require students to navigate a reading comprehension section in order to assess their reading ability, and it is probably this part of any standardized test that strikes the most fear into the hearts and minds of educators. That is because we know that reading is not only difficult to teach, but also difficult to learn, and that the ability for a student to truly comprehend what they have read depends upon them mastering a complex set of skills. So let's be clear. There is no strategy that can help a poor reader do well on a standardized test. The strategies we will speak of here are intended to be useful to those students who read at or above their grade level.

One of the most effective things you can do for your students is to clue them into the types of questions that they will encounter on a reading comprehension test. The elimination of the element of surprise will go a long way in helping your students do their best.

Reading comprehension tests usually contain literal, inferential, and analytical questions about both fiction and nonfiction passages.

- **Literal Questions:** These kinds of questions require you to recall or locate a detail which appears in the passage. The best strategy to use here is to simply go back to the passage and find the information.

- **Inferential Questions:** These kinds of questions require you to make a deduction, to read between the lines of a passage, or to look for information that may be unstated. To answer these types of questions, you have to use clues from the passage along with what you know in order to arrive at the correct answer.

- **Analytical Questions:** These types of questions require you to rely more on your own experience than the passage itself in order to arrive at the correct answer. Analytical questions often involve examining the author's purpose or point of view.

Use the following story and practice test during whole-group instruction. Have students practice answering reading comprehension questions and identifying the types of questions being posed.

Reading Comprehension Test Practice

Mercury and the Woodman
by Aesop

A woodman was chopping down a tree on the bank of a river. His axe accidentally flew out of his hands and fell into the water. The woodman was upset that he lost his axe. Suddenly, Mercury appeared and asked him why he was so upset. The woodman told Mercury what happened. Mercury felt sorry for the man so he dove into the river and brought up a golden axe. He asked the woodman if this was the one he had lost. The woodman said that it was not. Mercury dove a second time and brought up a silver axe. He asked the woodman if this was his axe. "No, that is not mine either," said the woodman. Once more Mercury dove into the river and brought up the missing axe. The woodman was happy at getting his axe back. He thanked Mercury warmly. Mercury was so pleased with his honesty that he gave him the other two axes.

When the woodman told the story to his friends, one of them became jealous. He decided to try his luck for himself. So he went and began to chop a tree at the edge of the river. He let his axe drop into the water on purpose. Mercury appeared as before. When he found out that the man's axe fell in the river, he dove in and brought up a golden axe. The fellow cried, "That's mine. That's mine." He reached out his hand for the prize. Mercury was so disgusted at his dishonesty that he refused to give him the golden axe. He also refused to get the axe that he let fall into the stream.

Directions: Read each question and fill in the answer circle for your choice. After you have answered each question, think about whether the question is literal, inferential, or analytical.

1. How did the woodman lose his axe?
   - Ⓐ He threw it away because it was broken.
   - Ⓑ It accidentally flew out of his hand.
   - Ⓒ His jealous friend stole it from him.
   - Ⓓ Mercury stole it from him.

THINK! What kind of question is this?

_____

2. Mercury decides to help the woodman because
   - Ⓔ he loves him.
   - Ⓕ he owes him a favor.
   - Ⓖ he feels sorry for him.
   - Ⓗ he promised him that he would.

THINK! What kind of question is this?

The Organization of Fiction and Nonfiction

Another good strategy with which students should be familiar is remembering how both fiction and nonfiction are organized. This will help them when they are confronted by questions that ask them to locate main ideas, problems, solutions, and supporting details. By the intermediate and middle school grades, most students have internalized this structure, so here we are simply reminding them of what they already know.

Fiction:

- **The Beginning:** In most works of fiction, information about the main characters and setting comes at the beginning of the story.

- **The Middle:** In most works of fiction, information about the problem that the characters are trying to solve comes in the middle of the story.

- **The End:** In most works of fiction, information about how the characters solved their problems comes at the end of the story.

Nonfiction:

- **The Beginning:** In most works of nonfiction, the main idea (and topic sentence) can be found at the beginning of the selection.

- **The Middle:** In most works of nonfiction, elaboration of the main idea, in the form of supporting details, can be found in the middle of the selection.

- **The End:** In most works of nonfiction, a summary of the main idea can be found at the end of the selection.

Use the following fiction and nonfiction passages and practice tests during whole group instruction. Have students practice answering reading comprehension questions. Encourage them to justify their answers.

In Upper Saxony there is a town called Hamelin. It is located in the region of Kalenberg. Hamlin is located right where two large rivers join together.

In the year of 1384, this town was infested by so many rats that they ate all of the corn the people had been storing for the winter months. They tried everything to chase away the rats but nothing worked. One day a stranger came to town. He was taller than most men. He wore colorful clothes. He told the townspeople that he could get rid of the rats if they would pay him a fee. The townspeople agreed.

The stranger took a flute from his jacket. As soon as he started to play, all of the rats came out of their holes and followed him. The stranger led them straight to the river. The rats ran into the river and were drowned. When he returned he asked for his money. The townspeople refused to pay. The next day there was a fair in the town. The stranger waited for the older townspeople to go to church. He took out another flute and began to play a song. All the boys in town above the age of fourteen gathered around him. He led them to the neighboring mountain, named Kopfelberg. Underneath this mountain is a sewer for the town. It is also where criminals are executed. All of the boys disappeared and were never seen again. A young girl who was following them saw what happened and brought the news of it to the town.

Directions: Read the passage and then fill in the answer circles for your choices. Think about how you know which is the correct answer.

1. Where is this story set?
   - (A) Kopfelberg Mountain
   - (B) The town of Hamelin
   - (C) Weser
   - (D) Hamel

   THINK! How do I know?

2. Who is the main character in this story?
   - (E) a young girl
   - (F) the narrator
   - (G) the Pied Piper
   - (H) the boys

   THINK! How do I know?

3. The Pied Piper is described as being
   - (A) shorter than most men.
   - (B) rather plump.
   - (C) very devious.
   - (D) taller than most men.

   THINK! How do I know?

(GO)

4. What problem does the Pied Piper agree to solve?
  - Ⓔ to rid the town of the rats
  - Ⓕ to play the flute at festivals
  - Ⓖ to discipline the badly behaved boys
  - Ⓗ He doesn't agree to do anything.

THINK! How do I know?

5. How does the Pied Piper drown the rats?
  - Ⓐ He chases them into the water.
  - Ⓑ He lures them to the water.
  - Ⓒ He sets traps along the river.
  - Ⓓ He gathers them up in a sack.

THINK! How do I know?

6. What part do the townspeople play in the disappearance of the boys?
  - Ⓔ They round them up and take them away.
  - Ⓕ They refuse to pay the Pied Piper.
  - Ⓖ They have nothing to do with it.
  - Ⓗ They give the Pied Piper permission to take them away.

THINK! How do I know?

7. It is likely that the rats and the boys followed the Pied Piper because
  - Ⓐ they were not very bright.
  - Ⓑ they liked him.
  - Ⓒ he promised them something.
  - Ⓓ he had magical powers.

THINK! How do I know?

8. The theme of this story is
  - Ⓔ don't trust strangers.
  - Ⓕ honor your debts.
  - Ⓖ don't live in a town with rats.
  - Ⓗ don't listen to flute music.

THINK! How do I know?

Nonfiction Passage

The ground shakes when the crust of the Earth moves. This is called an earthquake. It can be caused by the crust sliding, volcanic bursts, or man-made explosions. Earthquakes that cause the most damage come from the crust sliding.

At first, the crust may only bend because of pushing forces. But when the pushing becomes too much, the crust snaps and shifts into a new position. Shifting makes wiggles of energy that go out in all directions. This is like ripples when a stone is dropped in water. These are called *seismic waves*. The waves travel out from where the center of the earthquake is located. Sometimes people can hear these waves. This is because they make the whole planet ring like a bell. It must be awesome to hear this sound!

The crust moving may leave a crack, or fault, in the land. Geologists, scientists who study the Earth's surface, say that earthquakes often happen where there are old faults. There are weak places in the crust. Where there are faults, earthquakes may happen again and again.

Sometimes, when earthquakes happen under the ocean floor, they cause huge sea waves. These waves are called *tsunamis*. They can travel across the ocean as fast as 598 miles per hour. Tsunamis can produce waves over 49 feet high. During the 1964 Alaskan earthquake, giant waves caused most of the damage to the towns of Kodiak, Cordova, and Seward. Some waves raced across the ocean in the other direction to the coasts of Japan.

Although earthquakes are usually frightening, keep in mind that the distance to the center of the Earth is 3,960 miles. Most earthquakes begin less than 150 miles below the surface. Earthquakes are not a sign that the Earth is unsteady.

Directions: Read the passage and then fill in the answer circles for your choices. Think about how you know which is the correct answer.

1. Earthquakes are caused by
   - Ⓐ a giant sound beneath the ground.
   - Ⓑ explosions and the crust sliding.
   - Ⓒ volcanoes.
   - Ⓓ B and C
   - Ⓔ None of the above.

THINK! How do I know?

2. Huge waves that rush across the ocean can be caused by
   - Ⓕ tsunamis.
   - Ⓖ storms.
   - Ⓗ earthquakes beneath the ocean.
   - Ⓘ waves as high as 49 feet.

THINK! How do I know?

GO

Nonfiction Comprehension Questions *(cont.)*

3. Seismic waves are compared to

    Ⓐ ripples in water.

    Ⓑ a bell ringing.

    Ⓒ faults in the ground.

    Ⓓ none of these.

THINK! How do I know?

4. An effect of earthquakes is

    Ⓔ faults or cracks in the ground.

    Ⓕ pushing forces building up.

    Ⓖ an unsteady planet.

    Ⓗ a stone dropped in the water.

THINK! How do I know?

5. The author's purpose in this passage is

    Ⓐ to scare the reader.

    Ⓑ to inform the reader.

    Ⓒ to entertain the reader.

    Ⓓ to bore the reader.

THINK! How do I know?

6. When earthquakes happen under the ocean floor they sometimes cause

    Ⓔ tidal waves.

    Ⓕ jet stream.

    Ⓖ tsunamis.

    Ⓗ None of the above

THINK! How do I know?

7. You read in the newspaper that an old fault has been discovered nearby. What might happen?

    Ⓐ It will swallow you alive.

    Ⓑ An earthquake might happen there.

    Ⓒ A flood might happen there.

    Ⓓ Nothing would happen.

THINK! How do I know?

8. An appropriate title for this passage might be

    Ⓔ When Earthquakes Attack!

    Ⓕ Giant Waves from Nowhere

    Ⓖ How Earthquakes Happen

    Ⓗ The Mysteries of Our Earth

THINK! How do I know?

Language Arts: Complete Sentences

Directions: Fill in the correct answer circle which shows a complete sentence.

Sample

A.
- Ⓐ And then I fell off of my bike.
- Ⓑ Not even close to the finish line!
- Ⓒ **I deliver newspapers every day.**
- Ⓓ So loud I could barely think!

1.
- Ⓐ Is not a continent.
- Ⓑ Greenland a continent.
- Ⓒ The teacher said, "Greenland."
- Ⓓ Below freezing temperatures.

2.
- Ⓔ For many years.
- Ⓕ Decades ago, the United States experienced a population surge.
- Ⓖ Baby Boomers and their offspring.
- Ⓗ During post-World War II.

3.
- Ⓐ During hibernation an animal's pulse slows down.
- Ⓑ The pulse is a measure of.
- Ⓒ During the winter months, raccoons.
- Ⓓ On stored fat reserves.

4.
- Ⓔ The Empire State Building.
- Ⓕ Was once the world's tallest structure.
- Ⓖ New York is called "The Empire State."
- Ⓗ Located in Manhattan.

5.
- Ⓐ Genes are.
- Ⓑ Hereditary means that genes.
- Ⓒ From the mother and father.
- Ⓓ People inherit one gene from each parent.

Language Arts: Complete Sentences *(cont.)*

6.

- (E) An ecosystem is all the living and nonliving things in an area.
- (F) The planet is one large.
- (G) Deserts, forests and ponds are examples of.
- (H) The health of an ecosystem.

7.

- (A) The flow of heat.
- (B) Conduction means that heat flows from one object to another.
- (C) Convection means that heat.
- (D) Chicks sitting on eggs is an example of.

8.

- (E) Planet Earth is the third planet from the sun.
- (F) The gas giants.
- (G) Between the asteroid belt.
- (H) In an irregular orbit.

9.

- (A) Newton's laws explained.
- (B) Newton's second law states that.
- (C) During the Renaissance.
- (D) Sir Isaac Newton developed three laws of motion.

10.

- (E) Condensation and the water cycle.
- (F) Evaporation and condensation.
- (G) Evaporation, condensation, and collection are parts of the water cycle.
- (H) The water cycle.

Language Arts: Types of Sentences

Directions: Read each sentence. Fill in the answer circle that tells what type of sentence it is.

Sample

A. A stimulus is a change in the environment.

   Ⓐ **declarative**   Ⓒ exclamatory

   Ⓑ interrogative   Ⓓ imperative

---

1. Which parts of the body are part of the central nervous system?

   Ⓐ declarative   Ⓒ exclamatory

   Ⓑ interrogative   Ⓓ imperative

2. The spinal chord and the brain are part of the central nervous system.

   Ⓔ declarative   Ⓖ exclamatory

   Ⓕ interrogative   Ⓗ imperative

3. Wear a helmet when you ride a bike.

   Ⓐ declarative   Ⓒ exclamatory

   Ⓑ interrogative   Ⓓ imperative

4. Which system controls hormones?

   Ⓔ declarative   Ⓖ exclamatory

   Ⓕ interrogative   Ⓗ imperative

5. Wear protective goggles when you do yard work.

   Ⓐ declarative   Ⓒ exclamatory

   Ⓑ interrogative   Ⓓ imperative

6. The cerebrum is the biggest part of the brain.

   Ⓔ declarative   Ⓖ exclamatory

   Ⓕ interrogative   Ⓗ imperative

7. Watch out for that ball!

   Ⓐ declarative   Ⓒ exclamatory

   Ⓑ interrogative   Ⓓ imperative

8. A neuron is another name for a nerve cell.

   Ⓔ declarative   Ⓖ exclamatory

   Ⓕ interrogative   Ⓗ imperative

9. How does information travel to the brain?

   Ⓐ declarative   Ⓒ exclamatory

   Ⓑ interrogative   Ⓓ imperative

10. Be more careful when you play baseball.

   Ⓔ declarative   Ⓖ exclamatory

   Ⓕ interrogative   Ⓗ imperative

STOP

Language Arts: Subjects and Predicates

Directions: Read each sentence. Fill in the answer circle that tells whether the underlined part is the simple or complete subject or predicate.

Sample

A. <u>Jill, Sam and Pete</u> are competing in the finals.

    Ⓐ simple subject   **Ⓒ complete subject**

    Ⓑ simple predicate   Ⓓ complete predicate

---

1. The children <u>ran</u> down the street after the ice cream truck.

    Ⓐ simple subject   Ⓒ complete subject

    Ⓑ simple predicate   Ⓓ complete predicate

2. Before school he had to <u>make his bed and wash the breakfast dishes</u>.

    Ⓔ simple subject   Ⓖ complete subject

    Ⓕ simple predicate   Ⓗ complete predicate

3. The Statue of Liberty and the United Nations <u>are</u> both located in New York City.

    Ⓐ simple subject   Ⓒ complete subject

    Ⓑ simple predicate   Ⓓ complete predicate

4. There were <u>five dogs and seven cats</u> up for adoption.

    Ⓔ simple subject   Ⓖ complete subject

    Ⓕ simple predicate   Ⓗ complete predicate

5. Number eight <u>crossed the finished line in record time</u>!

    Ⓐ simple subject   Ⓒ complete subject

    Ⓑ simple predicate   Ⓓ complete predicate

(GO)

6. <u>The restaurant's specialty</u> is frog's legs.
    Ⓔ simple subject   Ⓖ complete subject
    Ⓕ simple predicate   Ⓗ complete predicate

7. It <u>took</u> him three days to memorize his lines for the play.
    Ⓐ simple subject   Ⓒ complete subject
    Ⓑ simple predicate   Ⓓ complete predicate

8. <u>The rules</u> say that if you roll a nine you lose a turn.
    Ⓔ simple subject   Ⓖ complete subject
    Ⓕ simple predicate   Ⓗ complete predicate

9. The band <u>learned a new song for the show</u>.
    Ⓐ simple subject   Ⓒ complete subject
    Ⓑ simple predicate   Ⓓ complete predicate

10. The map <u>showed</u> the most direct route to the beach.
    Ⓔ simple subject   Ⓖ complete subject
    Ⓕ simple predicate   Ⓗ complete predicate

Language Arts:
Independent and Dependent Clauses

Directions: Read each sentence. Fill in the answer circle that tells whether the underlined part is an independent or dependent clause.

Sample

A. John <u>had</u> a parrot that was blue and gold.

- Ⓐ independent
- **Ⓑ dependent**

---

1. <u>Sally was great at math</u>, and she was also good at science.
   - Ⓐ independent
   - Ⓑ dependent

2. When I use the phone <u>I make sure to speak quietly</u>.
   - Ⓒ independent
   - Ⓓ dependent

3. <u>If you run too fast</u>, you might not be able to finish the race.
   - Ⓐ independent
   - Ⓑ dependent

4. Emily and Sue were good friends and <u>they were also neighbors</u>.
   - Ⓒ independent
   - Ⓓ dependent

5. <u>My teacher asked a question</u> and then she called on Janice.
   - Ⓐ independent
   - Ⓑ dependent

6. <u>For the past two years</u>, I have gotten colds during the summertime.
   - Ⓒ independent
   - Ⓓ dependent

7. I went to my friend's party <u>and then to the movies</u>.
   - Ⓐ independent
   - Ⓑ dependent

8. If you like science fiction books, then <u>you might also like science fantasy books</u>.
   - Ⓒ independent
   - Ⓓ dependent

9. <u>Because I did so well in hockey</u>, I think I may also be good at playing baseball.
   - Ⓐ independent
   - Ⓑ dependent

10. I made the soup, and <u>my mother made the salad</u>.
    - Ⓒ independent
    - Ⓓ dependent

Language Arts: Compound and Complex Sentences

Directions: Read each sentence and determine if it is a compound or complex sentence. Fill in the correct answer circle.

> ## Sample
> **A.** The conductor wore a tuxedo, and the players wore black and white.
> - Ⓐ **compound**
> - Ⓑ complex

1. The train stops in several towns, so the passengers can stretch their legs.
   - Ⓐ compound
   - Ⓑ complex

2. I will go to the mall this evening if I can get a ride.
   - Ⓒ compound
   - Ⓓ complex

3. Although the temperature reached 95 degrees, I still had to mow the grass.
   - Ⓐ compound
   - Ⓑ complex

4. When the Europeans came to the New World, they brought many diseases with them.
   - Ⓒ compound
   - Ⓓ complex

5. I'd like to go, but I have to finish my homework.
   - Ⓐ compound
   - Ⓑ complex

6. I went swimming, and I learned how to dive!
   - Ⓒ compound
   - Ⓓ complex

7. Make a sharp right turn here, but don't drive into the ditch.
   - Ⓐ compound
   - Ⓑ complex

8. Sam has to get his work done, or he won't be allowed to play in the game.
   - Ⓒ compound
   - Ⓓ complex

9. The hotel has a good restaurant, and it also has a big outdoor pool.
   - Ⓐ compound
   - Ⓑ complex

10. Because of the bad weather, the concert had to be cancelled.
    - Ⓒ compound
    - Ⓓ complex

Language Arts: Sentence Combining

Directions: Read each pair of sentences. Fill in the answer circle which shows the best way in which to combine them to make one sentence.

Sample

A. The flag is red, white, and blue. The flag has fifty stars.
- (A) The red, white, and blue flag 50 stars has.
- (B) Fifty stars the red, white, and blue flag has.
- (C) **The red, white, and blue flag has fifty stars.**

1. The dog is black. The dog has white patches.
- (A) The dog is black, and the dog has white patches.
- (B) The dog is black and has white patches.
- (C) White patches the black dog has.

2. It is hot today. It is humid today.
- (D) It is hot and humid today.
- (E) Hot and humid it is today.
- (F) Today it is hot and it is humid.

3. Jason won the foot race. Jason hurt his leg while winning the foot race.
- (A) Jason won the foot race and hurt his leg while winning the foot race.
- (B) The foot race Jason won while hurting his leg.
- (C) Jason won the foot race, but hurt his leg.

4. Yesterday I went to the mall. I bought two books and a pair of sandals.
- (D) Yesterday I went to the mall and bought two books and a pair of sandals.
- (E) Two books and a pair of sandals I bought at the mall yesterday.
- (F) At the mall yesterday I bought two books and a pair of sandals.

5. I have to study for my social studies test. I have to do ten math problems.
- (A) Ten math problems and study for my social studies test I have to.
- (B) I have to study for my social studies test and then I have to do ten math problems.
- (C) I have to study for my social studies test and do ten math problems.

(GO)

Language Arts: Sentence Combining *(cont.)*

6. Jupiter is a gas giant. Jupiter is the fifth planet from the sun.
  - Ⓓ A gas giant, Jupiter is the fifth planet from the sun.
  - Ⓔ The fifth planet from the sun is a gas giant, Jupiter.
  - Ⓕ Jupiter, a gas giant, is the fifth planet from the sun.

7. The students left the building. The fire alarm rang this morning.
  - Ⓐ Students left the building this morning, and the fire alarm rang.
  - Ⓑ The fire alarm rang this morning, and the students left the building.
  - Ⓒ This morning, students left the building and the fire alarm rang.

8. I love to dance. I have been taking lessons for many years.
  - Ⓓ I love to dance and have been taking lessons for many years.
  - Ⓔ For many years lessons I have been taking and I love to dance.
  - Ⓕ I love to dance and for years I have been taking lessons.

9. I got lost on my way to the store. A neighbor gave me directions.
  - Ⓐ I got lost on my way to the store, but a neighbor gave me directions.
  - Ⓑ Directions a neighbor gave, and I got lost on the way to the store.
  - Ⓒ To the store I got lost, and a neighbor gave me directions.

STOP

Language Arts: Plural Nouns

Directions: Read each boldfaced word. Fill in the circle which shows the correct plural form of this word.

Sample

A. woman

  Ⓐ womans   **Ⓒ women**

  Ⓑ womens   Ⓓ woman

---

1. church

Ⓐ churches

Ⓑ churchs

Ⓒ church's

Ⓓ chetch

2. ax

Ⓔ axie

Ⓕ axs

Ⓖ axes

Ⓗ axis

3. tomato

Ⓐ tomatoes

Ⓑ tomatos

Ⓒ tomatoties

Ⓓ tomatoos

4. foot

Ⓔ foots

Ⓕ footies

Ⓖ feet

Ⓗ foot

5. shelf

Ⓐ shelfs

Ⓑ shelves

Ⓒ shelvies

Ⓓ shelvexes

6. piano

Ⓔ piano

Ⓕ piani

Ⓖ pianoies

Ⓗ pianos

7. loaf

Ⓐ loaves

Ⓑ loafs

Ⓒ loaffies

Ⓓ loaf

8. tariff

Ⓔ tarrifs

Ⓕ tarrifes

Ⓖ tarrffexes

Ⓗ tariffs

STOP

Language Arts: Possessive Nouns

Directions: Read each boldfaced phrase. Fill in the answer circle that shows the correct possessive form of the nouns.

Samples

A. the milk of the cow
- Ⓐ the cows' milk
- Ⓑ the cows milk
- **Ⓒ the cow's milk**

B. the paws of the kittens
- **Ⓓ the kittens' paws**
- Ⓔ the kitten's paw
- Ⓕ the kitten's paws

---

1. the mitten of the child
- Ⓐ the childs' mitten
- Ⓑ the child's mitten
- Ⓒ the children's mitten

6. the climate of the jungle
- Ⓓ the jungle's climate
- Ⓔ the jungles' climates
- Ⓕ the jungle's climates

---

2. the wind of the storm
- Ⓓ the storm's wind
- Ⓔ the storms' wind
- Ⓕ the storm's winds

7. the school for actors
- Ⓐ the actor's school
- Ⓑ the actors' school
- Ⓒ the actors school

---

3. the lounge of the teachers
- Ⓐ the teacher's lounge
- Ⓑ the teachers lounges
- Ⓒ the teachers' lounge

8. the groceries of the stores
- Ⓓ the store's groceries
- Ⓔ the store groceries
- Ⓕ the stores' groceries

---

4. the performers of the circus
- Ⓓ the circus's performers
- Ⓔ the circus'es performers
- Ⓕ the circus' performer's

9. the book of the student
- Ⓐ the student's book
- Ⓑ the students' book
- Ⓒ the student books

---

5. the meeting of the chefs
- Ⓐ the chef's meetings
- Ⓑ the chef's meeting
- Ⓒ the chefs' meeting

10. the characters in the play
- Ⓓ the plays' characters
- Ⓔ the play's character's
- Ⓕ the play's characters

Language Arts: Sentence Punctuation

Directions: Read each sentence. Fill in the answer circle that shows the sentence which is punctuated correctly.

Sample

A. Ⓐ John please pick up your toys?

Ⓑ John, please pick up your toys.

Ⓒ John…please pick up your toys.

---

1. Ⓐ The band rehearsals are on Mondays Wednesdays and Fridays.

   Ⓑ The band rehearsals, are on Mondays Wednesdays and Fridays.

   Ⓒ The band rehearsals are on Mondays, Wednesdays, and Fridays.

2. Ⓓ Mr. Jones can may I have tissue?

   Ⓔ Mr. Jones, may I have a tissue?

   Ⓕ Mr. Jones – may I have a tissue?

3. Ⓐ The test was on multiplication division and problem solving?

   Ⓑ The test was on multiplication division, and problem solving.

   Ⓒ The test was on multiplication, division, and problem solving.

4. Ⓓ Remember to clean your room, Linda.

   Ⓔ Remember, to clean your room, Linda!

   Ⓕ Remember…to clean your room Linda.

5. Ⓐ Franklin said "An apple a day keeps the doctor away."

   Ⓑ Franklin said, An apple a day keeps the doctor away.

   Ⓒ Franklin said, "An apple a day keeps the doctor away."

6. Ⓓ Tyrone can I borrow your bike?

   Ⓔ Tyrone: can I borrow your bike?

   Ⓕ Tyrone, can I borrow your bike?

7. Ⓐ Her symptoms were a sore throat, runny nose, and a headache.

   Ⓑ Her symptoms were a sore throat runny nose, and a headache.

   Ⓒ Her symptoms were a sore throat, runny nose, and a headache!

8. Ⓓ Mrs. Cohen, may I ask another question.

   Ⓔ Mrs. Cohen may I ask another question.

   Ⓕ Mrs. Cohen, may I ask another question?

Language Arts: Action and Linking Verbs

Directions: Read each sentence. Fill in the answer circle that identifies either the action verb or the linking verb.

Samples

A. My sister is great at basketball! (linking verb)

- (A) **is**
- (B) at
- (C) great

B. Carlos runs really fast! (action verb)

- (D) Carlos
- (E) **runs**
- (F) really

1. The lions are being fed at the moment. (linking verb)
   - (A) being
   - (B) are
   - (C) moment

2. Martin scrambled two eggs for breakfast. (action verb)
   - (D) Martin
   - (E) for
   - (F) scrambled

3. It seems that it has been raining forever! (linking verb)
   - (A) has
   - (B) seems
   - (C) been

4. She sneezed so loudly we heard her down the hall. (action verb)
   - (D) we
   - (E) hall
   - (F) sneezed

5. I don't think I will attend this year. (action verb)
   - (A) I
   - (B) think
   - (C) this

6. I will be happy when the test is over. (linking verb)
   - (D) be
   - (E) happy
   - (F) over

7. They worked very hard on the science project. (action verb)
   - (A) hard
   - (B) worked
   - (C) very

8. The United States is located on the continent of North America. (linking verb)
   - (D) located
   - (E) continent
   - (F) is

9. The students giggled at the teacher's joke. (action verb)
   - (A) joke
   - (B) the
   - (C) giggled

10. The puppy was being very mischievous. (linking verb)
    - (D) puppy
    - (E) being
    - (F) very

STOP

Language Arts: Verb Tense

Directions: Read each sentence. Fill in the answer circle that tells the tense of the underlined word or words.

Samples

A. I <u>will do</u> my chores tomorrow.
- (A) past
- (B) present
- (C) **future**

B. They <u>played</u> for two hours.
- (D) **past**
- (E) present
- (F) future

---

1. Kevin and Manuel <u>went</u> home early.
- (A) past
- (B) present
- (C) future

2. She <u>will be</u> there at two o'clock.
- (D) past
- (E) present
- (F) future

3. He <u>works</u> at the movie theater.
- (A) past
- (B) present
- (C) future

4. Thomas Jefferson <u>was</u> the third president.
- (D) past
- (E) present
- (F) future

5. They <u>will introduce</u> themselves when they arrive.
- (A) past
- (B) present
- (C) future

6. She <u>lifts</u> weights to stay in shape.
- (D) past
- (E) present
- (F) future

7. They <u>painted</u> the entire barn.
- (A) past
- (B) present
- (C) future

8. Dickens <u>wrote</u> many novels.
- (D) past
- (E) present
- (F) future

9. Their behavior <u>will affect</u> everyone.
- (A) past
- (B) present
- (C) future

10. He <u>is</u> very tall.
- (D) past
- (E) present
- (F) future

STOP

Language Arts: Verb Tense II

Directions: Read each sentence. Fill in the answer circle that tells the tense of the underlined word or words.

Samples

A. She <u>was playing</u> in the park.
- Ⓐ **past progressive**
- Ⓑ present progressive
- Ⓒ future perfect

B. She <u>has decided</u> on a red car.
- Ⓓ future perfect
- Ⓔ **present perfect**
- Ⓕ past perfect

---

1. Mike <u>has gone</u> to all of the meetings about the new park.
   - Ⓐ past
   - Ⓑ present perfect
   - Ⓒ past progressive

6. He <u>is driving</u> slowly because he doesn't want to miss the turn.
   - Ⓓ present progressive
   - Ⓔ past perfect
   - Ⓕ past progressive

---

2. They <u>will have worked</u> nine hours by day's end.
   - Ⓓ future
   - Ⓔ future progressive
   - Ⓕ future perfect

7. By the month's end, I <u>will have joined</u> two study groups.
   - Ⓐ future progressive
   - Ⓑ future perfect
   - Ⓒ present perfect

---

3. She rode her bike after she <u>had completed</u> all of her homework.
   - Ⓐ past perfect
   - Ⓑ past progressive
   - Ⓒ past

8. The cat <u>was climbing</u> the tree so quickly that you could barely see him.
   - Ⓓ past progressive
   - Ⓔ past
   - Ⓕ past perfect

---

4. Mrs. Marvel <u>is studying</u> for the trivia competition every day.
   - Ⓓ past progressive
   - Ⓔ present progressive
   - Ⓕ future progressive

9. She <u>has changed</u> her position often.
   - Ⓐ present perfect
   - Ⓑ past perfect
   - Ⓒ present progressive

---

5. Before the end of the year they <u>had collected</u> over two thousand dollars for the charity.
   - Ⓐ past
   - Ⓑ past perfect
   - Ⓒ past progressive

10. By next Monday, the committee <u>will have amended</u> the rules.
   - Ⓓ future perfect
   - Ⓔ future
   - Ⓕ present progressive

Language Arts: Vocabulary

Directions: Read each sentence. Fill in the answer circle that best tells the definition of the underlined word.

Sample

A. The clown's <u>trousers</u> were purple and red.

  Ⓐ shirt   Ⓑ shorts   **Ⓒ pants**   Ⓓ jacket

---

1. She would like to <u>adopt</u> a kitten.
   - Ⓐ buy
   - Ⓑ abandon
   - Ⓒ nurture
   - Ⓓ acquire

2. Sammy is determined to <u>conquer</u> his fear of flying.
   - Ⓔ give in to
   - Ⓕ defeat
   - Ⓖ strengthen
   - Ⓗ study

3. The <u>delta</u> is very fertile.
   - Ⓐ river's source
   - Ⓑ river's banks
   - Ⓒ an isthmus
   - Ⓓ area located at a river's mouth

4. England has had a <u>monarch</u> for hundreds of years.
   - Ⓔ king or queen
   - Ⓕ president
   - Ⓖ tribal chief
   - Ⓗ none of these

5. Because Juan could speak Spanish, he could <u>interpret</u> what the man was saying.
   - Ⓐ read
   - Ⓑ translate
   - Ⓒ use sign language
   - Ⓓ all of these

6. Our teacher said the process was called <u>photosynthesis</u>.
   - Ⓔ the process by which film is developed
   - Ⓕ the process by which water is recycled
   - Ⓖ the process by which plants make food
   - Ⓗ the process by which inertia is created

7. <u>Evaporation</u> is part of the water cycle.
   - Ⓐ when water condenses in to a liquid
   - Ⓑ when water condenses into ice
   - Ⓒ transpiration
   - Ⓓ when water condenses into vapor

8. The play was so long there was a fifteen minute <u>intermission</u>.
   - Ⓔ break
   - Ⓕ lecture
   - Ⓖ standing ovation
   - Ⓗ none of these

9. The congresswoman nodded her <u>assent</u>.
   - Ⓐ disapproval
   - Ⓑ disagreement
   - Ⓒ disgust
   - Ⓓ approval

10. His argument was completely <u>irrational</u>.
    - Ⓔ understandable
    - Ⓕ clear and concise
    - Ⓖ lacking reason and logic
    - Ⓗ well founded

(STOP)

Language Arts: Direct and Indirect Objects

Directions: Read each sentence. Fill in the answer circle that tells either the direct or indirect objects.

Sample

A. John hit the ball so hard that he broke his bat. (DO)

    Ⓐ John   Ⓑ his bat   Ⓒ **the ball**   Ⓓ so hard

---

1. Juan sent his grandmother a birthday card yesterday. (DO)

    Ⓐ Juan
    Ⓑ his grandmother
    Ⓒ a birthday card
    Ⓓ yesterday

2. Her story about the raccoon was published in a collection for children. (IO)

    Ⓔ short story collection for children
    Ⓕ her story
    Ⓖ published
    Ⓗ was

3. Keisha named her new puppy Wallace. (DO)

    Ⓐ Keisha
    Ⓑ her
    Ⓒ puppy
    Ⓓ Wallace

4. I recently read an article about the impact of global warming on glaciers. (DO)

    Ⓔ an article
    Ⓕ I recently
    Ⓖ global warming on glaciers
    Ⓗ none of these

5. My neighbor sold me his bike because he got a new one. (IO)

    Ⓐ me
    Ⓑ his bike
    Ⓒ My neighbor
    Ⓓ sold

6. I saw a huge reticulated python at the zoo. (DO)

    Ⓔ I
    Ⓕ huge
    Ⓖ zoo
    Ⓗ python

7. Our math teacher gave us a very difficult test today. (IO)

    Ⓐ us
    Ⓑ test
    Ⓒ math teacher
    Ⓓ our

8. Kwami loves to sled down that big hill around the corner! (DO)

    Ⓔ Kwami
    Ⓕ hill
    Ⓖ corner
    Ⓗ none of these

9. I received over one hundred dollars for my birthday. (IO)

    Ⓐ birthday
    Ⓑ one hundred dollars
    Ⓒ I
    Ⓓ my

10. Can you please give me a call when you arrive home? (DO)

    Ⓔ arrive home
    Ⓕ you
    Ⓖ when
    Ⓗ call

STOP

Language Arts: Subject Complements

Directions: Read each sentence. Fill in the answer circle that tells either the predicate noun (PN) or the predicate adjective (PA).

Sample
A. My mother is a great Italian cook. (PN)
- (A) mother
- (C) Italian
- **(B) cook**
- (D) none of these

---

1. The tree was nearly a hundred feet tall. (PN)
- (A) tree
- (B) a hundred feet tall
- (C) the
- (D) was

2. My dad's new car was fire engine red. (PA)
- (E) my dad's car
- (F) car
- (G) was
- (H) fire engine red

3. The book had a surprise ending. (PN)
- (A) had
- (B) the book
- (C) a surprise ending
- (D) a

4. Mandy's costume was too big for her, so she had to have it altered. (PA)
- (E) big
- (F) costume
- (G) Mandy's costume
- (H) it

5. The pizza smells great! (PA)
- (A) pizza
- (B) smells
- (C) great
- (D) the

6. We looked at the map to try to find our way to the carnival. (PN)
- (E) map
- (F) looked
- (G) we
- (H) our

7. Mr. Johnston was really eager for us to compete in the spelling bee. (PA)
- (A) eager
- (B) spelling bee
- (C) compete
- (D) us

8. The book is all about pirates and how they found a sunken treasure. (PN)
- (E) the book
- (F) treasure
- (G) they
- (H) pirates

9. That roller coaster was so scary I can hardly wait to go on again! (PA)
- (A) scary
- (B) roller coaster
- (C) wait
- (D) go on

10. We waited for the bus for nearly two hours before it finally came. (PN)
- (E) waited
- (F) bus
- (G) hours
- (H) came

STOP

Language Arts: Adjectives

Directions: Read each word. Fill in the answer circle that shows either the comparative or superlative form of the adjective.

Sample

A. easy (comparative)
- Ⓐ **easier**
- Ⓑ easiest

B. nice (superlative)
- Ⓒ nicer
- Ⓓ **nicest**

---

1. clever (comparative)
- Ⓐ most clever
- Ⓑ more clever

7. funny (comparative)
- Ⓐ funnier
- Ⓑ funniest

---

2. good (superlative)
- Ⓒ better
- Ⓓ best

8. bad (superlative)
- Ⓒ worst
- Ⓓ less worse

---

3. happy (comparative)
- Ⓐ happier
- Ⓑ most happy

9. solid (comparative)
- Ⓐ most solid
- Ⓑ more solid

---

4. generous (superlative)
- Ⓒ more generous
- Ⓓ most generous

10. little (superlative)
- Ⓒ less
- Ⓓ least

---

5. good (comparative)
- Ⓐ best
- Ⓑ better

11. beautiful (comparative)
- Ⓐ more beautiful
- Ⓑ most beautiful

---

6. many (superlative)
- Ⓒ more
- Ⓓ most

12. red (superlative)
- Ⓒ reddest
- Ⓓ less red

STOP

Language Arts: Adverbs

Directions: Find the adverb in each sentence. Fill in the correct answer circle.

Sample

A. Tomorrow I will begin my cooking class.

Ⓐ I   Ⓒ cooking

Ⓑ tomorrow   Ⓓ my

---

1. The juggler carefully balanced the red ball on the tip of his nose.

Ⓐ juggler

Ⓑ nose

Ⓒ balanced

Ⓓ carefully

2. I recently had my wisdom teeth removed.

Ⓔ I

Ⓕ recently

Ⓖ removed

Ⓗ none of the above

3. How soon will it be before we arrive?

Ⓐ soon

Ⓑ will

Ⓒ it

Ⓓ arrive

4. The cheetah moved in quickly for the kill.

Ⓔ cheetah

Ⓕ moved

Ⓖ kill

Ⓗ none of the above

5. My brother broke his collar bone yesterday.

Ⓐ broke

Ⓑ his

Ⓒ brother

Ⓓ yesterday

6. I happily volunteered to help the teacher.

Ⓔ happily

Ⓕ volunteered

Ⓖ help

Ⓗ the

7. I accidentally bumped my head on the ceiling of the car.

Ⓐ accidentally

Ⓑ my

Ⓒ bumped

Ⓓ of

8. She came around the corner so quickly, she nearly fell off her bike.

Ⓔ she

Ⓕ nearly

Ⓖ quickly

Ⓗ both F and G

9. The plane landed so smoothly that I didn't even wake up!

Ⓐ landed

Ⓑ plane

Ⓒ up

Ⓓ smoothly

10. I seldom go to bed before 11 o'clock.

Ⓔ I

Ⓕ go

Ⓖ to

Ⓗ none of the above

STOP

Language Arts: Pronouns

Directions: Read each sentence. Find the pronoun that can best replace the underlined part of each sentence.

Sample

A. <u>Steve, Janice, and Fred</u> all went downtown to see the play.

   Ⓐ **They**   Ⓒ She

   Ⓑ Them   Ⓓ Us

---

1. Give the book to <u>Mary</u> when you are finished reading it.
   Ⓐ her
   Ⓑ she
   Ⓒ him
   Ⓓ it

2. <u>My mother and I</u> went to visit the home of Thomas Jefferson in Virginia.
   Ⓔ they
   Ⓕ we
   Ⓖ them
   Ⓗ none of these

3. Can somebody please help <u>Mrs. Anderson</u> sort the papers?
   Ⓐ her
   Ⓑ she
   Ⓒ him
   Ⓓ he

4. <u>The plate</u> fell onto the floor and broke into a million pieces.
   Ⓔ he
   Ⓕ it
   Ⓖ we
   Ⓗ they

5. They gave the award to <u>Mike, José, and me</u>.
   Ⓐ we
   Ⓑ them
   Ⓒ she
   Ⓓ us

6. <u>The ball</u> was passed to Jackson.
   Ⓔ him
   Ⓕ he
   Ⓖ they
   Ⓗ none of these

7. <u>My ancestors</u> are from Italy.
   Ⓐ they
   Ⓑ them
   Ⓒ us
   Ⓓ we

8. <u>The pie</u> was so delicious I wanted to order a second piece!
   Ⓔ they
   Ⓕ it
   Ⓖ you
   Ⓗ them

9. Did Kathy tell <u>Ronald</u> about the science project?
   Ⓐ she
   Ⓑ her
   Ⓒ him
   Ⓓ none of these

10. <u>The orchestra</u> played beautifully.
    Ⓔ them
    Ⓕ those
    Ⓖ us
    Ⓗ they

STOP

Language Arts: Pronoun Referents

Directions: Read each sentence carefully. Fill in the answer circle that names the person, place, or thing to which the underlined pronoun refers.

1. Mrs. Washington was so frustrated with her students that she kept <u>them</u> in for lunch.
   - Ⓐ Mrs. Washington
   - Ⓑ lunch
   - Ⓒ students
   - Ⓓ was

2. The United States celebrated <u>its</u> bicentennial in 1976.
   - Ⓔ United States
   - Ⓕ celebrated
   - Ⓖ bicentennial
   - Ⓗ it

3. The students completed their work early, so Mr. Fredericks let <u>them</u> play chess.
   - Ⓐ chess
   - Ⓑ work
   - Ⓒ Mr. Fredericks
   - Ⓓ students

4. Jamal told Tamika that he'd loan <u>her</u> ten dollars, so she could buy the book.
   - Ⓔ loan
   - Ⓕ dollars
   - Ⓖ Tamika
   - Ⓗ book

5. This medial procedure was considered the first of <u>its</u> kind.
   - Ⓐ medical procedure
   - Ⓑ kind
   - Ⓒ this
   - Ⓓ was

GO

6. When Tanya won the race, <u>she</u> was overjoyed.

- Ⓔ she
- Ⓕ Tanya
- Ⓖ race
- Ⓗ the

7. I asked my friend George if <u>he</u> wanted to join the softball team.

- Ⓐ George
- Ⓑ friend
- Ⓒ softball
- Ⓓ team

8. A common misconception about bears is that <u>they</u> are man-eaters.

- Ⓔ misconception
- Ⓕ bears
- Ⓖ man-eaters
- Ⓗ about

9. After Sharon returned from vacation, <u>she</u> was very energetic.

- Ⓐ Sharon
- Ⓑ vacation
- Ⓒ returned
- Ⓓ was

10. Skateboarding is difficult because <u>it</u> requires great balance.

- Ⓔ difficult
- Ⓕ balance
- Ⓖ great
- Ⓗ skateboarding

(STOP)

Language Arts: Prepositional Phrases

Directions: Read each sentence carefully. Fill in the answer circle that shows the prepositional phrase.

Sample

A. I left my library books on the top shelf of the coatroom closet.

    Ⓐ I left my library books   **Ⓒ on the top shelf of the coatroom closet**

    Ⓑ the coatroom closet   Ⓓ none of these

---

1. You have to chose between chocolate or vanilla ice-cream.

    Ⓐ you have to

    Ⓑ chose between

    Ⓒ chocolate or vanilla ice-cream

    Ⓓ between chocolate or vanilla ice-cream

---

2. I went to the movies instead of the park.

    Ⓔ I went to

    Ⓕ the movies

    Ⓖ the park

    Ⓗ instead of the park

---

3. I saw three baby chicks swimming down in the river.

    Ⓐ down in the river

    Ⓑ I saw three baby chicks

    Ⓒ swimming down

    Ⓓ none of these

---

4. In front of the library there is a statue of Ben Franklin.

    Ⓔ a statue of Ben Franklin

    Ⓕ in front of the library

    Ⓖ there is a

    Ⓗ none of these

---

5. During the assembly I had a sneezing fit.

    Ⓐ had a sneezing fit

    Ⓑ assembly I had

    Ⓒ during the assembly

    Ⓓ I had a

GO

6. I live around the corner from my best friend Robert.

- (E) around the corner
- (F) my best friend
- (G) I live around
- (H) none of these

7. The public pool is located across the street from the grocery store.

- (A) the public pool
- (B) is located across
- (C) from the grocery store
- (D) none of these

8. I suspected that the magician was doing something to the cards underneath the table.

- (E) I suspected that
- (F) underneath of the table
- (G) the magician was doing
- (H) none of these

9. I feel confident about all of my tests except for science.

- (A) I feel confident
- (B) about all of my tests
- (C) except for science
- (D) none of these

10. Sammy threw the ball so hard it landed across the street from his house.

- (E) across the street
- (F) Sammy threw the ball
- (G) so hard it
- (H) none of these

Language Arts: Contractions

Directions: Fill in the answer circle that shows the correct contraction.

Sample

A. he will

  Ⓐ heal   Ⓒ it'll

  Ⓑ he'll   Ⓓ we'll

---

1. I am

  Ⓐ Ia'm

  Ⓑ it's

  Ⓒ I'm

  Ⓓ I'd

2. would not

  Ⓔ wouldn't

  Ⓕ won't

  Ⓖ weren't

  Ⓗ we'll

3. I would

  Ⓐ I'll

  Ⓑ it's

  Ⓒ I'd

  Ⓓ isn't

4. they are

  Ⓔ they've

  Ⓕ they're

  Ⓖ there

  Ⓗ their

5. have not

  Ⓐ hasn't

  Ⓑ he'll

  Ⓒ hadn't

  Ⓓ haven't

6. you are

  Ⓔ your

  Ⓕ you've

  Ⓖ you're

  Ⓗ yo'ure

7. are not

  Ⓐ aren't

  Ⓑ are'nt

  Ⓒ isn't

  Ⓓ weren't

8. should have

  Ⓔ shan't

  Ⓕ she's

  Ⓖ should've

  Ⓗ shouldn't

STOP

Language Arts: Mixed Practice

Directions: Read each sentence carefully. Then read the boldfaced questions. Follow the instructions and fill in the correct answer circle.

Sample
A. My mother said, Please clean your room! **What is this sentence missing?**

Ⓐ a comma   Ⓒ a capital letter

Ⓑ quotation marks   Ⓓ a semicolon

1. The courses offered are the following biology, music, theater, and dance.
   What is this sentence missing?
   Ⓐ semicolon
   Ⓑ colon
   Ⓒ comma
   Ⓓ quotation marks

2. Hey, wait for me!
   Which word is the interjection?
   Ⓔ wait
   Ⓕ me
   Ⓖ hey
   Ⓗ for

3. My brother Jake just turned twenty one years old.
   Between which two words would you place a hyphen?
   Ⓐ brother and Jake
   Ⓑ years and old
   Ⓒ just and turned
   Ⓓ twenty and one

4. I warned my sister about leaving the windows open but she didn't listen.
   What is this sentence missing?
   Ⓔ a period
   Ⓕ a comma
   Ⓖ a colon
   Ⓗ The sentence is grammatically correct.

5. Juana and Maria are Identical twins.
   What is wrong with this sentence?
   Ⓐ The word "twins" should be capitalized.
   Ⓑ There should be a hyphen between the words "Identical" and "twins."
   Ⓒ The word "identical" should not be capitalized.
   Ⓓ There is nothing wrong with the sentence.

6. Shelia bought two pairs of shoes and a new scarf.
   Which word is the conjunction?
   Ⓔ and
   Ⓕ of
   Ⓖ scarf
   Ⓗ a

7. I really love to draw drawing is my passion.
   This sentence needs a semi-colon. Where would you place it?
   Ⓐ after the word is
   Ⓑ after the word love
   Ⓒ after the word draw
   Ⓓ after the word drawing

8. Rachel asked, Do you want to come to my birthday party?
   What is wrong with this sentence?
   Ⓔ It should end with an exclamation point
   Ⓕ It is too long.
   Ⓖ It has no predicate.
   Ⓗ It needs quotation marks

Language Arts: Reading Comprehension

Directions: Read each passage carefully. Fill in the correct answer circle.

Food in Ancient Egypt

In Ancient Egypt, as in most societies, the more money you had, the better you ate. Even so, all Egyptians practiced the habit of sitting or half-kneeling on the floor while they ate, their knees tucked under them. Sometimes guests at parties sat at their own small table in the homes of the rich and were served by slaves. But they too ate with their fingers like everyone else, rinsing their hands with water.

Royalty ate from dishes made of gold and silver. Less wealthy diners had to be content with dishes made of marble, alabaster, limestone, and rock crystal. Favorite expensive foods included ox meat, duck, wildfowl, and desert game such as Oryx or gazelle, basted in honey and seasoned with parsley and cilantro. Lumps of fat in radish oil flavored with juniper berries might be sprinkled with cumin and served beside bowls of brown beans and chickpeas. Fresh celery, leeks, and lettuce complemented bread that came with plates of olive oil for dipping. Grapes, honey, cakes, heads of roasted garlic, and figs were delicacies. Finally, large wine jars, labeled by vineyard and vintage year, were present at banquets, as was beer.

The poor prayed for eternal nourishment in the afterlife, naming bread and beer, different kinds of wildfowl, and fruit. But, in fact, most of those were not often available to them while they lived. Meat was scarce because it was expensive. Bread and beer were common, but the meals of the poor usually consisted of what they planted or raised on their own: onions, leeks, beans, and lentils. For special occasions, a tasty dish was sesame seed paste mixed with spices and oil, mopped from a bowl with pieces of bread. Egyptians could fish in the Nile, of course, but many would not eat fish because they thought it was unlucky.

(GO)

1. How did the ancient Egyptians eat?
   - (A) standing at tables
   - (B) sitting at tables
   - (C) sitting on the floor
   - (D) laying down

2. Why do you think guests ate at their own tables?
   - (E) The Egyptians really didn't like having guests to dinner.
   - (F) The table manners of the guests had to be assessed before they could eat with the group.
   - (G) as a sign of respect
   - (H) none of these

3. Why do you think the ancient Egyptians ate with their hands?
   - (A) They didn't have good manners.
   - (B) Utensils probably were not invented yet.
   - (C) It made the food taste better.
   - (D) none of these

4. What does "vintage year" mean in paragraph two?
   - (E) the current year
   - (F) the year the winemaker was born
   - (G) the year the vines were planted
   - (H) the year the wine was made

5. What did poor Egyptians eat on special occasions?
   - (A) beer
   - (B) fish
   - (C) sesame seed paste
   - (D) leeks

6. Why didn't many Egyptians eat fish?
   - (E) They didn't like fish.
   - (F) Fish were expensive.
   - (G) They thought fish were unlucky.
   - (H) The Nile only contains poisonous fish.

7. What is cumin?
   - (A) a spice
   - (B) a type of cheese
   - (C) a type of bird
   - (D) none of these

8. If your dinner plate was made of marble, it probably meant that you were what?
   - (E) wealthy
   - (F) a special guest
   - (G) royalty
   - (H) poor

STOP

Language Arts: Reading Comprehension

Directions: Read each passage carefully. Fill in the correct answer circle.

Jabberwocky
by
Lewis Carroll

'Twas brillig, and the slithy toves
Did gyre and gimble in the wabe:
All mimsy were the borogoves,
And the mome raths outgrabe.

"Beware the Jabberwock, my son!
The jaws that bite, the claws that catch!
Beware the Jubjub bird, and shun
The frumious Bandersnatch!"

He took his vorpal sword in hand:
Long time the manxome foe he sought—
So rested he by the Tumtum tree,
And stood awhile in thought.

And, as in uffish thought he stood,
The Jabberwock, with eyes of flame,
Came whiffling through the tulgey wood,
And burbled as it came!

One, two! One, two! And through and through
The vorpal blade went snicker-snack!
He left it dead, and with its head
He went galumphing back.

"And hast thou slain the Jabberwock?
Come to my arms, my beamish boy!
O frabjous day! Callooh! Callay!"
He chortled in his joy.

'Twas brillig, and the slithy toves
Did gyre and gimble in the wabe:
All mimsy were the borogoves,
And the mome raths outgrabe.

1. What did the slithy toves do in the wabe?
   Ⓐ outgrade
   Ⓑ gyre and gimble
   Ⓒ mimsey
   Ⓓ snicker-snack

2. What is a Jabberwock?
   Ⓔ a kind of fairy
   Ⓕ a kind of monster
   Ⓖ a kind of wizard
   Ⓗ none of these

3. What kind of sound did the vorpol blade make?
   Ⓐ burble
   Ⓑ Callooh
   Ⓒ snicker-snack
   Ⓓ Callay

4. How does the poet describe the Bandersnatch?
   Ⓔ mimsy
   Ⓕ tulgey
   Ⓖ uffish
   Ⓗ frumious

GO

Language Arts: Reading Comprehension *(cont.)*

The Sixth Grade Nickname Game
By
Gordon Korman

What's in a nickname? A lot, as the undisputed champion nicknamers, Wiley and Jeff, of Old Orchard Public School (OOPS) find out. On a bet, they dub a bashful kid Iceman, claiming that unless a nickname is precisely right, it won't stick. Instead, Iceman's popularity soars. Jeff and Wiley are also baffled by a new girl in class, Cassandra, whose uniqueness defies easy nicknames. It's Cassandra who leads the charge to raise the class's reading scores in an attempt to save the job of their beloved substitute, a high-school-football-coach-turned-elementary-teacher, Mr. Hughes — Mr. Huge, as the students nickname him. "I've had a lot of teachers," says one respectfully, "but Mr. Huge is the only one who can push a bus." He is also a tireless cheerleader for his students. He hoots and war-dances in class, exhorting his kids to give 110 percent and become all-stars, MVPs, and academic Hall of Famers. But Jeff and Wiley find their eleven-year friendship strained to the limit over their shared fascination with Cassandra, ending in a ridiculous fistfight inside a horse costume before hundreds of parents. Korman indulges his deadpan humor (the Iceman's reply to every desperate letter in his school newspaper advice column is "I don't know") and a liking for odd similes ("silence fell over the room like a drape on a birdcage") in this funny parable about the power of positive thinking, and a point worth remembering — that the only good nickname is a flattering one.

Review by Charles Shields

---

5. Who is the author of the book?
   Ⓐ Charles Shields
   Ⓑ Gordon Korman
   Ⓒ Jeff Wiley
   Ⓓ Cassandra

6. What is the summary of the plot of the book?
   Ⓔ A girl named Cassandra leads a revolt against a teacher.
   Ⓕ Two boys learn that nicknames don't really describe everything about a person.
   Ⓖ A class gets in big trouble when it scores poorly on a test.
   Ⓗ A kid nicknamed "the Iceman" surprises everyone.

7. Which of the following is true?
   Ⓐ Mr. Hughes is a pro teacher.
   Ⓑ Wiley and Jeff become jealous over Cassandra.
   Ⓒ The nickname "Iceman" embarrasses a boy.
   Ⓓ This is a serious book about problems in school.

8. What is the reviewer's opinion of *The 6th Grade Nickname Game?*
   Ⓔ Not very much happens in the book.
   Ⓕ The author's writing doesn't make sense.
   Ⓖ The title of the book is unclear.
   Ⓗ The book makes a good point.

Directions: Read each passage carefully. Fill in the correct answer circle.

How the Mentally Ill Were Treated: Ancient Greece Through the Middle Ages

Mental illness is not a modern disease. Mental illness has been part of the human story since ancient times. Literature and historical documents from a long time ago make that clear,.

Mental illness was called *madness* or *insanity*. These terms are no longer used because they are too broad. In addition, what seems mad to one society may not seem so to another. The Greek historian Herodotus, writing in the mid-5th century B.C., argued that King Cambyses of Persia was mad, because he made fun of holy services honoring the gods and mocked tradition. Today such behavior might draw criticism, but it wouldn't be viewed as mental illness.

In Ancient Greece and Rome, it was the custom of families to take responsibility for mentally ill relatives. Legal means were available to prevent mentally disabled persons from ruining the family's property or finances. But institutions set aside for their care were almost unknown. Usually, the mentally ill roamed the streets and the countryside. Often, they were mistreated. People pelted them with stones or spat at them to drive them away. Nearly everyone believed that madness was contagious.

Christianity became the official religion of the Roman Empire in the 4th century A.D., but attitudes about insanity changed very little. On the one hand, the Christian emphasis on charity towards others was of some benefit. On the other hand, fear of evil and demons also whipped up superstitions. Because of this, the Middle Ages in Europe saw the rise of witch hunts. No doubt many of the women accused of witchcraft were mentally ill. Their crimes may have been defending themselves with curses and threats. Fears linking evil with madness were also at the root of witch hysteria in colonial New England in the 1600s.

By contrast, the Muslim world responded sympathetically to persons with mental diseases. The Islamic holy book, *The Koran*, laid down the principle that society was responsible for the weak and sick. The Muslim influence in Spain led to the founding of hospitals for the mentally ill in the 14th and 15th centuries. Juan Cuidad Duarte, who had experienced a breakdown early in life, later founded the religious Order of the Hospitaler. The order built hospitals for the insane in Spain, Italy, and France. In London, St. Mary of Bethlehem Hospital, founded in 1247, included those who had *fallen out of their wits*.

Overall, societies in the Middle Ages coped with mentally ill people poorly. Madmen's huts and towers offered shelter. More often, local officials forced out mentally disabled wanderers. If they returned, they were whipped. If they returned a second time, they were beaten. Some towns in Germany hired sailors to take the mentally ill off their hands, giving rise to the phrase *ship of fools*. Where these ships sailed and what happened to the passengers is not known.

(GO)

1. Why are the terms "madness" and "insanity" no longer used?
   Ⓐ They are offensive.
   Ⓑ They are too broad.
   Ⓒ They only describe illness in ancient times.
   Ⓓ none of these

2. Why did Herodotus think that Cambyses was insane?
   Ⓔ Because he had hallucinations.
   Ⓕ Because he was unconventional.
   Ⓖ Because he was a very bad king.
   Ⓗ Because he had a breakdown.

3. How did Christianity fuel fear of the mentally ill?
   Ⓐ It made people more charitable towards others.
   Ⓑ It preached fear of the mentally ill.
   Ⓒ It stirred up belief in evil and demons.
   Ⓓ none of these

4. How did Muslim societies view the mentally ill?
   Ⓔ with ambivalence
   Ⓕ with hatred
   Ⓖ with fear
   Ⓗ with sympathy

5. Why do you think that Juan Cuidad Duarte was interested in helping the mentally ill?
   Ⓐ He was a good Muslim.
   Ⓑ He father was mentally ill.
   Ⓒ He was a skilled psychiatrist.
   Ⓓ He suffered a breakdown in his youth.

STOP

The Iceman

During a few days of unusually warm weather in 1993, hikers in the Tyrolean Alps—a mountain range that borders Italy and Austria—came upon a startling sight. Trapped in the melting ice and snow was the body of a man. Police were summoned to the scene, but soon the authorities realized that this was not a case of a recent hiker who had lost his way. The Iceman, as newspapers called him, is the oldest and best-preserved human body ever found.

Careful examination by anthropologists showed that the wind and cold had dried the flesh like a mummy's. He had been a man in midlife, about 5' 3" tall and weighing 110 pounds. His dark hair and beard were cut short. On his skin were mysterious marks: tattoos that might have been medicine magic to help relieve pains in his joints. The condition of his spine pointed to a bad back. His legs showed signs of strain, and his nose was squashed like a boxer's. He had lived a hard life.

But how long ago had he journeyed into the Alps? Radiocarbon tests conducted on his body and tools—including the grains of grass pollen found on his wool clothing—indicated that the Ice man had lived before Mohammed, Christ, or Buddha. He was at least 5,000 years old!

Specialists in prehistory returned to the place where his body and scattered artifacts had been discovered, searching for clues about his final hours. Perhaps he was lost or trying to escape enemies pursuing him. A snowstorm forced him to take shelter in a natural trench six feet deep and 20 feet wide. Under the lip of the trench, he stashed his equipment—his backpack, tools, and copper axe—and settled in to wait out the storm. As it grew colder, he probably pulled his woven grass cape tightly around him and prepared a fire from live coals he kept in a birch-bark cylinder.

His last meal was a handful of sloe berries and meat from a tough alpine goat—an ibex. Beside him was his powerful bow: nine feet long and capable of blowing a hole through a deer's chest cavity from 30 yards away. For some reason, however, he left it unstrung, the bowstring curled up neatly in a pouch. Perhaps he knew there would be no hunting so high up among the treeless boulders.

The storm continued, and finally, despite his efforts to stay alive, the Iceman died from the freezing cold. His body lay buried under snow for years. Then a glacier, moving slowly over the centuries, sealed the trench shut, preserving the wanderer and all of his belongings in a natural time capsule.

The world that the Iceman left behind was harsh and dangerous, made a little easier by advances in farming. It was an age of faith in warlike gods, of terror and death by starvation, or attack from bands of strangers. It was a world where people like the Iceman had to rely on their tribes and themselves. And despite the glimpses into prehistoric times that the discovery of his body had provided, one key question remains: Who was he? A wandering trader, a prospector, an outcast? Was he chased into the mountains for breaking the law of some kind? Or was he a leader who had climbed the mountains to find new opportunities for his people?

So much has been learned about the Iceman and his final hours, but his identity will probably remain a secret forever.

(GO)

6. In what year was the Iceman discovered?
- Ⓔ 1990
- Ⓕ 1993
- Ⓖ 2007
- Ⓗ 1983

7. Who did police initially think the Iceman was?
- Ⓐ a caveman
- Ⓑ a escaped convict
- Ⓒ a lost hiker
- Ⓓ none of these

8. What evidence was there that the Iceman had lived a hard life?
- Ⓔ He left a diary.
- Ⓕ His legs were broken.
- Ⓖ There were calluses on his hands.
- Ⓗ His legs showed strain and his nose was squashed.

9. What kept the Iceman so perfectly preserved?
- Ⓐ He was sealed in an icy trench for thousands of years.
- Ⓑ He was wrapped in woven clothing.
- Ⓒ He was covered by the bones of an ibex.
- Ⓓ none of these

10. How did anthropologists determine the age of the Iceman?
- Ⓔ x-rays
- Ⓕ autopsy
- Ⓖ radiocarbon tests
- Ⓗ all of these

11. Where was the Iceman found?
- Ⓐ the United States
- Ⓑ Russia
- Ⓒ the Tyrolean Alps
- Ⓓ Africa

12. What were the mysterious marks on the Iceman?
- Ⓔ bite wounds
- Ⓕ tattoos for relieving pain
- Ⓖ moles
- Ⓗ freckles

(STOP)

Language Arts: Essay Test

Directions: Read each topic carefully. Write a persuasive essay that takes a firm position either for or against the given topic.

Topic #1: In many states it is now illegal to talk on a cell phone while driving a car. In most cases, however, police officers do not have the right to pull drivers over unless they are doing something else illegal in addition to talking on a cell phone. Do you think that police officers should have the right to pull drivers over for talking on a cell phone only?

Topic #2: In an attempt to promote healthy eating, your school is considering removing any and all lunch menu items that contain trans fat, sugar, and caffeine. This would include the removal of such items as soda, candy, pizza, hamburgers, and grilled cheese, to name a few. Do you think your school has a right to impose a healthy diet on its middle school students, or should the students have a right to choose?

Topic #3: Many adults often feel that violence in some video games and in the lyrical content of some popular music adversely affects young people. Do you think that listening to violent lyrics and playing violent video games can make a young person violent?

Topic #4: In order to address bullying in school, some administrators are considering implementing a strict no-bullying policy. The policy is a three-strikes model, meaning that if the same person is caught bullying on three separate occasions, they will be expelled from school. Do you think this policy will reduce and/or eliminate bullying in school?

Topic #5: A newspaper recently reported that a boy of the age of fifteen committed a homicide while robbing a small grocery store. If he is tried as an adult and found guilty he could either face the death penalty or life imprisonment. Do you think the boy should be tried as an adult?

Topic #6: Many products that people use, including cosmetics, shampoos, perfumes, and medicines are developed by performing tests on animals like cats, dogs, and rabbits. Some of these tests are painful, and sometimes the animals die as a result of the tests. Should people be permitted to perform any tests they want on animals, or should there be restrictions on the types of tests to which animals are subjected?

Standardized Math Test Strategies

While many of the same strategies that students use to navigate other portions of standardized tests apply to math tests, there are a few additional methods with which they should be familiar. Math, after all, is an animal all its own and routinely requires students to solve a plethora of problems by applying a variety of problem solving strategies.

✓ **Know the Vocabulary!** Make sure you are familiar with all of the related terms that may appear on the test. Area, circumference, and quotient: It would be a shame to get a problem wrong simply because you didn't understand what you were being asked to do!

✓ **Underline Key Words!** Read the problem carefully, then underline the key words that indicate what you are required to find. Are you looking for the sum? The difference? The perimeter?

✓ **Recognize and Eliminate the Unnecessary!** Often math word problems will provide you with information that you don't need in order to solve the problem. Seek the information you need and ignore the information you don't.

✓ **Select a Strategy!** Often there is more than one way to solve a problem. Choose the strategy which will work best for you. Will you draw a picture? Use a formula? Make a graph?

✓ **Use Estimation and Recognition!** In many cases you will be able to recognize the correct answer immediately. In others, you may be able to simply make an estimate. Estimation and recognition are two strategies that can save you a lot of time on standardized tests.

✓ **Use Mental Math!** Occasionally, you may encounter problems that you can solve in your head. Lucky you! This, too, can save you a lot of time.

✓ **Read all of the Options!** Before you jump to any conclusions, make sure that you read all of the options. Think of the options as helping hands leading you to the correct answer.

✓ **Beware of the Lure!** You may frequently encounter traps or lures on multiple-choice math exams. Often one of the options, usually the first or second one will contain an answer that appears correct but is actually wrong. Have a look:

> **If you add $ 11.11 to $ 32.73 the sum will be**
> Ⓐ $43.84 greater than $32.73. (*lure*)   Ⓒ $11.11 less than $32.73 (*incorrect*)
> Ⓑ $43.84 less than $32.73   (*lure*)   Ⓓ $43.84   (*correct*)

This is your average, run-of-the-mill addition problem. However, if you were not careful, you might be tricked into selecting either A or B because the first number that you see, $ 43.84, is actually the sum of $32.73 and $11.11. Of course, neither one of these is the correct answer.

✓ **Use All of the Time!** It's never a good idea to rush through any test, but math tests in particular require that you check and double-check your work. If you have time, go back over as many problems as you can to make sure that your answers are correct.

Mathematics: Decimal Forms

Directions: Read each problem carefully. Fill in the correct answer circle.

Sample

A. eight and nine tenths in decimal form

  Ⓐ **8.9**   Ⓑ .89   Ⓒ 8.09   Ⓓ 8.009

---

1. .329 in word form

  Ⓐ three and twenty-nine hundredths

  Ⓑ three hundred twenty-nine tenths

  Ⓒ three hundred twenty-nine thousandths

  Ⓓ three hundred and twenty-nine hundredths

---

2. four thousandths in decimal form

  Ⓔ .04

  Ⓕ .004

  Ⓖ 4.0

  Ⓗ .4

---

3. seven and two hundredths in decimal form

  Ⓐ 7.02

  Ⓑ .702

  Ⓒ 7.002

  Ⓓ none of these

---

4. 9.209 in word form

  Ⓔ nine and two thousand nine hundredths

  Ⓕ nine and two hundred nine thousandths

  Ⓖ nine and twenty-nine hundredths

  Ⓗ two hundred nine thousandths

---

5. forty-seven hundredths in decimal form

  Ⓐ .47

  Ⓑ .047

  Ⓒ 4.7

  Ⓓ none of these

GO

6. 3.9 in word form

    Ⓔ three and nine hundredths

    Ⓕ three and nine thousandths

    Ⓖ three point nine

    Ⓗ three and nine tenths

7. eight hundredths in decimal form

    Ⓐ .08

    Ⓑ .008

    Ⓒ .8

    Ⓓ 8.10

8. 17.002 in word form

    Ⓔ seventeen and two thousandths

    Ⓕ seventeen and two hundredths

    Ⓖ seventeen and two tenths

    Ⓗ seventeen point two hundredths

9. seventy-six hundredths in decimal form

    Ⓐ .076

    Ⓑ 7.6

    Ⓒ .76

    Ⓓ 7.76

10. .7 in word form

    Ⓔ seven tenths

    Ⓕ seven hundredths

    Ⓖ seven thousandths

    Ⓗ seven ten thousandths

STOP

Mathematics: Rounding Decimals

Directions: Read each problem carefully. Round to the boldfaced place value. Fill in the correct answer circle.

Samples

A. 7.0239
- (A) 7.0200
- **(B) 7.02**
- (C) 7.0009
- (D) 2.789

B. 2.789
- **(E) 2.79**
- (F) 2.800
- (G) 2.78
- (H) none of these

---

1. 93.46
- (A) 93
- (B) 94
- (C) 93.45
- (D) 93.40

2. 8.3005
- (E) 8.31
- (F) 8.00
- (G) 8.30
- (H) none of these

3. 714.9739
- (A) 714.975
- (B) 714.970
- (C) 714.974
- (D) 714.980

4. 47.09
- (E) 47.10
- (F) 48
- (G) 47
- (H) 47.08

5. 129.0789
- (A) 129.1
- (B) 129.1789
- (C) 129.17
- (D) 130

6. 9.2547
- (E) 9.256
- (F) 9.257
- (G) 10
- (H) 9.255

7. 506.9207
- (A) 506.91
- (B) 506.902
- (C) 506.92
- (D) none of these

8. 12.0734
- (E) 12.
- (F) 12
- (G) 12.08
- (H) none of these

STOP

Mathematics: Comparing and Ordering Decimals & Scientific Notation

Directions: For problems 1–4, order the decimals from greatest to least or from least to greatest. Fill in the correct answer circle.

Sample

A. From least to greatest: .709 .63 .0672 .9

   Ⓐ .9 .709 .63 .0672

   Ⓑ **0672 .63 .709 .9**

   Ⓒ .63 .9 .0672 .709

   Ⓓ none of these

---

1. From greatest to least:
  2.90 .2 2.09 .002

   Ⓐ 2.90 2.09 .2 .002

   Ⓑ 2.09 2.90 .002 .2

   Ⓒ .002 .2 2.09 2.90

   Ⓓ .2 2.09 2.90 .002

---

2. From greatest to least:
  3.09 .3 3.0907 3.02

   Ⓔ 3.02 3.09 3.0907

   Ⓕ 3.02 3.09 3.0907 .3

   Ⓖ 3.0907 3.09 3.02 .3

   Ⓗ none of these

---

3. From least to greatest:
  .7 .070 .007 .017

   Ⓐ .007 .017 .070 .7

   Ⓑ .7 .070 .017 .007

   Ⓒ .070 .017 .007 .7

   Ⓓ .7 .017 .070 .007

---

4. From least to greatest:
  2.007 2.01 2.76 2.2

   Ⓔ 2.76 2.2 2.01 2.007

   Ⓕ 2.01 2.2 2.76 2.01

   Ⓖ 2.007 2.01 2.2 2.76

   Ⓗ none of these

GO

Mathematics: Comparing and Ordering Decimals & Scientific Notation *(cont.)*

Directions: For problems 5 – 8 convert from standard form to scientific notation and vice versa.

Sample

B. 7.9 x 10 to the 8th

   Ⓐ 79,000,000

   Ⓑ 790,000,000,000

   Ⓒ **790,000,000**

   Ⓓ 7,000,000,000,000

---

5. 2.8 x 10 to the 5th

   Ⓐ 280,000

   Ⓑ 28,000,000

   Ⓒ 2,800,000

   Ⓓ none of these

6. 450,000,000,000

   Ⓔ 4.5 x 10 to the 10th

   Ⓕ 4.5 x 10 to the 9th

   Ⓖ 4.5 x 10 to the 11th

   Ⓗ 4.5 x 10 to the 12th

7. 9.3 x 10 to the 7th

   Ⓐ 93,000,000

   Ⓑ 930,000,000

   Ⓒ 9,300,000

   Ⓓ 930,000,000,000

8. 780,000,000

   Ⓔ 78 x 10 to the 8th

   Ⓕ 7.8 x 10 to the 10th

   Ⓖ 7.8 x 10 to the 12th

   Ⓗ 7.8 x 10 to the 8th

STOP

Mathematics: Addition and Subtraction of Decimals

Directions: Read each problem carefully. Fill in the correct answer circle.

Samples

A. 12.097 + .9023 =
- Ⓐ **12.9993**
- Ⓑ 21.119
- Ⓒ 130002
- Ⓓ 130,002

B. 20.786 – 2.342
- Ⓔ 18,444
- Ⓕ 184.44
- Ⓖ **18.444**
- Ⓗ 19.444

---

1. 4.0892 + 7.320 =
- Ⓐ 114, 092
- Ⓑ 11.4092
- Ⓒ 114.092
- Ⓓ 48.212

5. 2.907 – .9099 =
- Ⓐ 19971
- Ⓑ 19.971
- Ⓒ 199.71
- Ⓓ 1.9971

---

2. 12.8904 + .0763 =
- Ⓔ 1296.67
- Ⓕ 129.667
- Ⓖ 12.9667
- Ⓗ 13.9667

6. 215.45 – 214.0978 =
- Ⓔ 13.522
- Ⓕ 135.22
- Ⓖ 1.3522
- Ⓗ 13,522

---

3. 3.70 – .2379 =
- Ⓐ 3.4621
- Ⓑ 34.621
- Ⓒ 346.21
- Ⓓ 3462.1

7. 12.5590 + 2.6 =
- Ⓐ 15159
- Ⓑ 1.5159
- Ⓒ 15.159
- Ⓓ 15,159

---

4. 123.78 – .9974 =
- Ⓔ 12.27826
- Ⓕ 122.7826
- Ⓖ 12278.26
- Ⓗ 1.227826

8. .789 + .23 =
- Ⓔ 1.019
- Ⓕ 10.19
- Ⓖ 101.9
- Ⓗ .1019

STOP

Mathematics: Multiplying Decimals

Directions: Read each problem carefully. Fill in the correct answer circle.

Samples

A. 5.91 x .29 =
- (A) 17139
- (B) 17.139
- **(C) 1.7139**
- (D) none of these

B. 395 x .809 =
- (E) 319,555
- (F) 31,9555
- (G) 3.19555
- **(H) 319.555**

---

1. 21.09 x .092 =
- (A) 1.94028
- (B) 19.4028
- (C) 194.028
- (D) 19402.8

5. 7.6 x .0003 =
- (A) 02.28
- (B) 002.28
- (C) 022.8
- (D) 0.00228

---

2. 3.43 x .9 =
- (E) 308.7
- (F) 30.87
- (G) .3087
- (H) 3.087

6. 7.9 x .24 =
- (E) 189.6
- (F) 18.96
- (G) 1.896
- (H) .1896

---

3. 976 x 9.231 =
- (A) 9009.456
- (B) 9, 009, 456
- (C) .9009456
- (D) none of these

7. 23.098 x 37 =
- (A) 8.54626
- (B) 854.626
- (C) 8546.26
- (D) none of these

---

4. 9.670 x 1.235 =
- (E) 119.4245
- (F) 11.94245
- (G) 1194.245
- (H) 119424.5

8. 2.907 x 1.78 =
- (E) 517.446
- (F) 51.7446
- (G) 517446
- (H) none of these

STOP

Mathematics: Dividing Decimals

Directions: Read each problem carefully. Fill in the correct answer circle.

Samples

A. $7.2 \div 4 =$
- (A) 18
- (B) .18
- **(C) 1.8**
- (D) none of these

B. $2.52 \div 0.7 =$
- (E) 36
- **(F) 3.6**
- (G) .36
- (H) 0.36

---

1. $87.4 \div 3.8 =$
- (A) 2.3
- (B) .23
- (C) 23
- (D) .023

5. $4.984 \div 0.7 =$
- (A) 712
- (B) 7.12
- (C) 71.2
- (D) .712

---

2. $23.6 \div .4 =$
- (E) 59
- (F) 5.9
- (G) .59
- (H) 5.09

6. $13.932 \div 9 =$
- (E) 15.48
- (F) 154.8
- (G) 1,548
- (H) 1.548

---

3. $55.22 \div .35 =$
- (A) 157.77
- (B) 15.777
- (C) 1577.7
- (D) none of these

7. $2.035 \div 5 =$
- (A) 407
- (B) 40.7
- (C) 4.07
- (D) none of these

---

4. $62.995 \div .74$
- (E) 8513
- (F) 85.13
- (G) 851.1
- (H) 8, 513

8. $57.77 \div 10 =$
- (E) 5.777
- (F) .5777
- (G) 57.77
- (H) 577.7

STOP

Mathematics: Divisibility

Directions: Read each problem carefully. Fill in the correct answer circle.

Sample

A. Which number is 228 divisible by?

Ⓐ 7   Ⓒ 14

Ⓑ 10   **Ⓓ 2**

---

1. Which number is 68 divisible by?

Ⓐ 4

Ⓑ 6

Ⓒ 8

Ⓓ all of these

2. Which number is 549 divisible by?

Ⓔ 9

Ⓕ 10

Ⓖ 8

Ⓗ 5

3. Which number is 1,760 divisible by?

Ⓐ 15

Ⓑ 9

Ⓒ 10

Ⓓ 7

4. Which number is 4,938 divisible by?

Ⓔ 10

Ⓕ 4

Ⓖ 17

Ⓗ 2

5. Which number is 516 divisible by?

Ⓐ 7

Ⓑ 4

Ⓒ 19

Ⓓ 5

6. Which number is 249 divisible by?

Ⓔ 3

Ⓕ 9

Ⓖ 20

Ⓗ all of these

7. Which number is 45,120 divisible by?

Ⓐ 10

Ⓑ 4

Ⓒ 5

Ⓓ all of these

8. Which number is 6,168 divisible by?

Ⓔ 9

Ⓕ 10

Ⓖ 5

Ⓗ 2

STOP

Mathematics: Prime and Composite Numbers and Prime Factorization

Directions: Read each problem carefully. Fill in the correct answer circle.

Samples

A. Which is a prime number?
- Ⓐ 6
- **Ⓑ 7**
- Ⓒ 12
- Ⓓ 24

B. Which is a composite number?
- Ⓔ 13
- Ⓕ 7
- **Ⓖ 18**
- Ⓗ all of these

---

1. What is the prime factorization of 42?
- Ⓐ 2 x 3 x 7
- Ⓑ 2 x 2 x 7
- Ⓒ 2 x 10 x 2
- Ⓓ none of these

5. What is the prime factorization of 80?
- Ⓐ 2 x 2 x 2 x 5
- Ⓑ 2 x 2 x 2 x 2 x 5
- Ⓒ 2 x 2 x 2 x 2 x 2 x 5
- Ⓓ all of these

---

2. Which is a prime number?
- Ⓔ 54
- Ⓕ 36
- Ⓖ 97
- Ⓗ 72

6. Which is a composite number?
- Ⓔ 5
- Ⓕ 17
- Ⓖ 102
- Ⓗ 101

---

3. Which is a composite number?
- Ⓐ 29
- Ⓑ 7
- Ⓒ 15
- Ⓓ 67

7. Which is a prime number?
- Ⓐ 47
- Ⓑ 72
- Ⓒ 50
- Ⓓ all of these

---

4. What is the prime factorization of 96?
- Ⓔ 2 x 2 x 2 x 2 x 2 x 2 x 3
- Ⓕ 2 x 2 x 2 x 2 x 2 x 3
- Ⓖ 3 x 3 x 3 x 3 x 3 x 2
- Ⓗ none of these

8. What is the prime factorization of 77?
- Ⓔ 7 x 7 x 7 x 7
- Ⓕ 11 x 11 x 11
- Ⓖ 70 x 7
- Ⓗ 11 x 7

STOP

Mathematics: Least Common Multiples and Greatest Common Factors

Directions: Read each problem carefully. Fill in the correct answer circle.

Samples

A. find the LCM of 5 and 12.

- Ⓐ 16
- **Ⓑ 60**
- Ⓒ 24
- Ⓓ 120

B. Find the GCF of 20 and 30.

- **Ⓔ 10**
- Ⓕ 20
- Ⓖ 1
- Ⓗ 2

---

1. Find the GCF of 8 and 40.

- Ⓐ 10
- Ⓑ 9
- Ⓒ 8
- Ⓓ none of these

2. Find the LCM of 8 and 10.

- Ⓔ 10
- Ⓕ 40
- Ⓖ 36
- Ⓗ 80

3. Find the GCF of 12 and 27.

- Ⓐ 4
- Ⓑ 9
- Ⓒ 6
- Ⓓ 3

4. Find the LCM of 7 and 9.

- Ⓔ 7
- Ⓕ 9
- Ⓖ 60
- Ⓗ 63

5. Find the GCF of 48 and 36.

- Ⓐ 9
- Ⓑ 16
- Ⓒ 12
- Ⓓ none of these

6. Find the GCF of 8 and 27.

- Ⓔ 1
- Ⓕ 216
- Ⓖ 15
- Ⓗ 7

7. Find the LCM of 3 and 15.

- Ⓐ 15
- Ⓑ 30
- Ⓒ 12
- Ⓓ 2

8. Find the LCM of 9 and 20.

- Ⓔ 150
- Ⓕ 167
- Ⓖ 180
- Ⓗ 20

STOP

Mathematics: Fraction Concepts

Directions: Read each problem carefully. Fill in the correct answer circle.

<hr>

Samples

A. Which is equivalent of $\frac{10}{15}$?

  Ⓐ $\frac{12}{32}$ Ⓒ $\frac{20}{30}$

  Ⓑ $\frac{7}{10}$ Ⓓ none of these

B. Write $\frac{9}{12}$ in lowest terms.

  Ⓔ $\frac{3}{4}$ Ⓖ $\frac{18}{24}$

  Ⓕ $\frac{2}{8}$ Ⓗ $\frac{7}{10}$

<hr>

1. Which is equivalent to $\frac{3}{27}$?

  Ⓐ $\frac{2}{9}$ Ⓒ $\frac{1}{9}$

  Ⓑ $\frac{7}{9}$ Ⓓ none of these

2. Which is equivalent to $\frac{8}{10}$?

  Ⓔ $\frac{4}{5}$ Ⓖ $\frac{40}{50}$

  Ⓕ $\frac{16}{20}$ Ⓗ all of these

3. Write $\frac{14}{38}$ in lowest terms.

  Ⓐ $\frac{6}{19}$ Ⓒ $\frac{10}{10}$

  Ⓑ $\frac{7}{19}$ Ⓓ It is already in lowest terms.

4. Write $\frac{27}{36}$ in lowest terms.

  Ⓔ $\frac{9}{12}$ Ⓖ $\frac{7}{10}$

  Ⓕ $\frac{2}{10}$ Ⓗ $\frac{3}{4}$

5. Which is equivalent to $\frac{15}{36}$?

  Ⓐ $\frac{135}{324}$ Ⓒ $\frac{14}{97}$

  Ⓑ $\frac{5}{12}$ Ⓓ Both A and B

6. Write $\frac{12}{84}$ in lowest terms.

  Ⓔ $\frac{2}{7}$ Ⓖ $\frac{24}{108}$

  Ⓕ $\frac{1}{7}$ Ⓗ none of these

7. Which is equivalent to $\frac{6}{24}$?

  Ⓐ $\frac{8}{30}$ Ⓒ $\frac{17}{21}$

  Ⓑ $\frac{2}{8}$ Ⓓ $\frac{9}{30}$

8. Write $\frac{11}{88}$ in lowest terms.

  Ⓔ $\frac{1}{8}$ Ⓖ $\frac{10}{15}$

  Ⓕ $\frac{88}{176}$ Ⓗ none of these

STOP

Mathematics: Fraction Concepts II

Directions: Read each problem carefully. Write mixed numbers as improper fractions and write improper fractions as mixed numbers. Answers should be in lowest terms.

Samples

A. $4\frac{7}{8}$

    Ⓐ $\frac{32}{8}$ © $\frac{39}{8}$

    Ⓑ $\frac{19}{8}$ Ⓓ $\frac{12}{8}$

B. $\frac{52}{9}$

    Ⓔ $5\frac{2}{9}$ Ⓖ $5\frac{9}{9}$

    Ⓕ $5\frac{7}{9}$ Ⓗ none of these

---

1. $2\frac{9}{10}$

    Ⓐ $\frac{21}{10}$ © $\frac{21}{10}$

    Ⓑ $\frac{29}{10}$ Ⓓ $\frac{180}{10}$

2. $7\frac{18}{20}$

    Ⓔ $\frac{140}{20}$ Ⓖ $\frac{158}{20}$

    Ⓕ $\frac{158}{10}$ Ⓗ none of these

3. $\frac{67}{19}$

    Ⓐ $4\frac{10}{19}$ © $\frac{10}{19}$

    Ⓑ $3\frac{10}{19}$ Ⓓ $7\frac{10}{18}$

4. $\frac{112}{12}$

    Ⓔ $9\frac{4}{12}$ Ⓖ 9

    Ⓕ $9\frac{1}{4}$ Ⓗ $9\frac{1}{3}$

5. $4\frac{17}{32}$

    Ⓐ $\frac{145}{32}$ © $\frac{141}{32}$

    Ⓑ $\frac{53}{32}$ Ⓓ none of these

6. $\frac{97}{2}$

    Ⓔ $\frac{1}{2}$ Ⓖ $49\frac{1}{2}$

    Ⓕ $48\frac{1}{2}$ Ⓗ $48\frac{2}{3}$

7. $\frac{63}{27}$

    Ⓐ $2\frac{9}{27}$ © $2\frac{1}{3}$

    Ⓑ $2\frac{1}{2}$ Ⓓ none of these

8. $13\frac{5}{10}$

    Ⓔ $\frac{28}{10}$ Ⓖ $\frac{23}{10}$

    Ⓕ $\frac{135}{10}$ Ⓗ $\frac{130}{10}$

STOP

Mathematics: Converting Fractions and Decimals

Directions: Read each problem carefully. Write decimals as fractions and fractions as decimals. Fill in the correct answer circle.

Samples

A. 0.68

Ⓐ $\frac{68}{1000}$ 　Ⓑ $\frac{68}{100}$ 　Ⓒ $\frac{68}{10}$

B. $\frac{3}{4}$

Ⓓ **0.75** 　Ⓔ 07.5 　Ⓕ .75

---

1. $\frac{1}{8}$

Ⓐ .0125 　Ⓑ .125 　Ⓒ 12.5

6. .43

Ⓓ $\frac{43}{100}$ 　Ⓔ $\frac{43}{1000}$ 　Ⓕ $\frac{43}{10000}$

---

2. .3

Ⓓ $\frac{3}{100}$ 　Ⓔ $\frac{3}{10}$ 　Ⓕ $\frac{3}{1000}$

7. $\frac{9}{20}$

Ⓐ .045 　Ⓑ 4.5 　Ⓒ .45

---

3. $\frac{1}{3}$

Ⓐ 3 　Ⓑ .333 　Ⓒ 3.3

8. $\frac{7}{50}$

Ⓓ .014 　Ⓔ .14 　Ⓕ .0014

---

4. .409

Ⓓ $\frac{409}{100}$ 　Ⓔ $\frac{409}{10}$ 　Ⓕ $\frac{409}{1000}$

9. .0027

Ⓐ $\frac{27}{1000}$ 　Ⓑ $\frac{27}{10000}$ 　Ⓒ $\frac{27}{100}$

---

5. $\frac{3}{16}$

Ⓐ .1875 　Ⓑ .18.75 　Ⓒ 187.5

10. .2

Ⓓ $\frac{2}{100}$ 　Ⓔ $\frac{2}{10}$ 　Ⓕ $\frac{2}{1000}$

STOP

Mathematics: Comparing and Ordering Fractions and Decimals

Directions: Read each problem carefully. Find the series of fraction or decimals that is ordered from least to greatest. Fill in the correct answer circle.

Samples

A.

Ⓐ $\frac{1}{4}, \frac{5}{8}, \frac{5}{6}$ Ⓒ $\frac{5}{8}, \frac{1}{4}, \frac{5}{6}$

B.

Ⓓ .3, .032, .03   Ⓕ **.03, .3, 0.32**

Ⓑ $\frac{5}{6}, \frac{1}{4}, \frac{5}{8}$ Ⓔ 0.32, .03, .3

1.
Ⓐ $\frac{3}{6}, \frac{9}{12}, \frac{15}{18}$ Ⓑ $\frac{9}{12}, \frac{15}{18}, \frac{3}{6}$ Ⓒ $\frac{15}{18}, \frac{9}{12}, \frac{3}{6}$

2.
Ⓓ $\frac{3}{8}, \frac{2}{7}, \frac{3}{5}$ Ⓔ $\frac{2}{7}, \frac{3}{8}, \frac{3}{5}$ Ⓕ $\frac{3}{8}, \frac{2}{7}, \frac{3}{5}$

3.
Ⓐ $\frac{7}{12}, \frac{1}{5}, \frac{2}{9}$ Ⓑ $\frac{2}{9}, \frac{7}{12}, \frac{1}{5}$ Ⓒ $\frac{1}{5}, \frac{2}{9}, \frac{7}{12}$

4.
Ⓓ $\frac{1}{2}, \frac{9}{20}, \frac{3}{10}$ Ⓔ $\frac{9}{20}, \frac{1}{2}, \frac{3}{10}$ Ⓕ $\frac{3}{10}, \frac{9}{20}, \frac{1}{2}$

5.
Ⓐ $\frac{4}{5}, \frac{2}{8}, \frac{1}{3}$ Ⓑ $\frac{2}{8}, \frac{1}{3}, \frac{4}{5}$ Ⓒ $\frac{1}{3}, \frac{2}{8}, \frac{4}{5}$

6.
Ⓓ $\frac{5}{7}, \frac{4}{21}, \frac{2}{3}$ Ⓔ $\frac{4}{21}, \frac{5}{7}, \frac{2}{3}$ Ⓕ $\frac{4}{21}, \frac{2}{3}, \frac{5}{7}$

GO

7.

Ⓐ .017, .17, .7   Ⓑ .7, .17, .017   Ⓒ .017, .7, .17

8.

Ⓓ .90, .327, .4   Ⓔ .327, .4, .90   Ⓕ .4, .327, .90

9.

Ⓐ 4.70, .4008, 4.4   Ⓑ 4.4, .4008, 4.70   Ⓒ .4008, 4.4, 4.70

10.

Ⓓ .0302, .302, .32   Ⓔ .32, .0302, .302   Ⓕ .302, .32, .0302

11.

Ⓐ .77, .0777, .077   Ⓑ .077, .0777, .77   Ⓒ .0777, .077, .77

12.

Ⓓ 13.2, 13.003, 13.02   Ⓔ 13.02, 13.002, 13.2   Ⓕ 13.002, 13.02, 13.2

Mathematics: Adding and Subtracting Fractions

Directions: Read each problem carefully. Fill in the correct answer circle. All answers must be in lowest terms.

Samples

A.

$2\dfrac{3}{5} + 7\dfrac{7}{15} =$

  Ⓐ $9\dfrac{15}{16}$ Ⓒ $10\dfrac{1}{15}$

  Ⓑ $9\dfrac{1}{15}$ Ⓓ none of these

B.

$7\dfrac{11}{12} - 4\dfrac{1}{12} =$

  Ⓔ $3\dfrac{5}{6}$ Ⓖ $\dfrac{3}{5}$

  Ⓕ $3\dfrac{10}{12}$ Ⓗ none of these

1.

$6\dfrac{6}{24} - 5\dfrac{8}{12} =$

  Ⓐ $1\dfrac{14}{24}$ Ⓒ $\dfrac{7}{74}$

  Ⓑ $\dfrac{7}{12}$ Ⓓ none of these

5.

$12\dfrac{2}{9} + 2\dfrac{56}{72} =$

  Ⓐ 1 Ⓒ 15

  Ⓑ $14\dfrac{72}{72}$ Ⓓ 17

2.

$9\dfrac{9}{10} - 2\dfrac{11}{30} =$

  Ⓔ $\dfrac{46}{30}$ Ⓖ $1\dfrac{16}{30}$

  Ⓕ $4\dfrac{46}{30}$ Ⓗ $7\dfrac{8}{15}$

6.

$9\dfrac{7}{12} - 8\dfrac{9}{24} =$

  Ⓔ $\dfrac{29}{24}$ Ⓖ $\dfrac{5}{24}$

  Ⓕ $1\dfrac{5}{24}$ Ⓗ none of these

3.

$12\dfrac{32}{48} + 7\dfrac{2}{8} =$

  Ⓐ $\dfrac{44}{48}$ Ⓒ $20\dfrac{44}{48}$

  Ⓑ $19\dfrac{11}{12}$ Ⓓ none of these

7.

$14\dfrac{3}{9} + 7\dfrac{3}{7}$

  Ⓐ $21\dfrac{16}{21}$ Ⓒ $20\dfrac{48}{63}$

  Ⓑ $\dfrac{48}{63}$ Ⓓ none of these

4.

$3\dfrac{6}{16} + 1\dfrac{27}{80} =$

  Ⓔ $\dfrac{57}{80}$ Ⓖ $1\dfrac{57}{80}$

  Ⓕ $3\dfrac{57}{80}$ Ⓗ $4\dfrac{57}{80}$

8.

$7\dfrac{11}{12} - 2\dfrac{15}{36} =$

  Ⓔ $4\dfrac{54}{36}$ Ⓖ $1\dfrac{3}{6}$

  Ⓕ $1\dfrac{18}{36}$ Ⓗ none of these

STOP

Mathematics: Multiplying Fractions

Directions: Read each problem carefully. Fill in the correct answer circle. All answers must be in lowest terms.

Samples

A.

$\dfrac{7}{8} \times \dfrac{1}{2} =$

- Ⓐ 1
- Ⓒ $\dfrac{7}{16}$
- Ⓑ $\dfrac{8}{10}$
- Ⓓ $\dfrac{8}{16}$

B.

$2 \times \dfrac{3}{12} =$

- Ⓔ $\dfrac{1}{2}$
- Ⓖ $\dfrac{5}{12}$
- Ⓕ $\dfrac{6}{12}$
- Ⓗ $\dfrac{5}{13}$

1.

$2\dfrac{3}{7} \times 1\dfrac{4}{5} =$

- Ⓐ $\dfrac{340}{49}$
- Ⓒ $4\dfrac{13}{35}$
- Ⓑ $3\dfrac{7}{12}$
- Ⓓ $\dfrac{46}{49}$

5.

$\dfrac{2}{9} \times 3\dfrac{1}{3} =$

- Ⓐ 4
- Ⓒ $\dfrac{20}{12}$
- Ⓑ $\dfrac{20}{27}$
- Ⓓ $\dfrac{20}{36}$

2.

$5 \times 3\dfrac{2}{5} =$

- Ⓔ $\dfrac{85}{5}$
- Ⓖ $\dfrac{4}{9}$
- Ⓕ 20
- Ⓗ 17

6.

$7\dfrac{9}{10} \times 4\dfrac{2}{7} =$

- Ⓔ $33\dfrac{6}{7}$
- Ⓖ $1\dfrac{60}{70}$
- Ⓕ $\dfrac{6}{7}$
- Ⓗ none of these

3.

$3\dfrac{2}{3} \times 4\dfrac{1}{12} =$

- Ⓐ $14\dfrac{35}{36}$
- Ⓒ $\dfrac{35}{36}$
- Ⓑ $\dfrac{539}{36}$
- Ⓓ none of these

7.

$\dfrac{2}{9} \times 9$

- Ⓐ $\dfrac{18}{9}$
- Ⓒ $1\dfrac{2}{11}$
- Ⓑ $\dfrac{11}{9}$
- Ⓓ 2

4.

$4\dfrac{7}{10} \times 7 =$

- Ⓔ $\dfrac{329}{10}$
- Ⓖ 33
- Ⓕ $\dfrac{9}{10}$
- Ⓗ $32\dfrac{9}{10}$

8.

$8\dfrac{2}{3} \times 1\dfrac{1}{2} =$

- Ⓔ $\dfrac{78}{6}$
- Ⓖ 12
- Ⓕ $9\dfrac{78}{6}$
- Ⓗ none of these

STOP

Mathematics: Dividing Fractions

Directions: Read each problem carefully. Fill in the correct answer circle. All answers must be in lowest terms.

Samples

A.

$$\frac{2}{9} \div \frac{7}{8} =$$

Ⓐ $\frac{14}{72}$ Ⓒ $\frac{14}{70}$

Ⓑ $\frac{9}{17}$ Ⓓ $\frac{16}{63}$

B.

$$2\frac{3}{4} \div 7\frac{1}{2} =$$

Ⓔ $\frac{22}{60}$ Ⓖ $\frac{13}{19}$

Ⓕ $\frac{11}{30}$ Ⓗ $\frac{22}{60}$

1.

$$2\frac{1}{2} \div 3\frac{1}{3} =$$

Ⓐ $\frac{12}{20}$ Ⓒ $5\frac{3}{5}$

Ⓑ $\frac{3}{4}$ Ⓓ none of these

2.

$$4 \div \frac{2}{3} =$$

Ⓔ $\frac{8}{3}$ Ⓖ 6

Ⓕ $\frac{6}{3}$ Ⓗ $\frac{12}{2}$

3.

$$2\frac{1}{10} \div \frac{3}{4} =$$

Ⓐ $\frac{12}{15}$ Ⓒ $2\frac{4}{5}$

Ⓑ $2\frac{12}{15}$ Ⓓ $2\frac{24}{30}$

4.

$$\frac{9}{10} \div \frac{7}{12} =$$

Ⓔ 1 Ⓖ $\frac{19}{35}$

Ⓕ $1\frac{19}{35}$ Ⓗ none of these

5.

$$\frac{2}{8} \div 7\frac{1}{2} =$$

Ⓐ $\frac{1}{30}$ Ⓒ $2\frac{1}{8}$

Ⓑ $\frac{2}{112}$ Ⓓ none of these

6.

$$4\frac{1}{4} \div 4 =$$

Ⓔ 4 Ⓖ $4\frac{2}{4}$

Ⓕ 5 Ⓗ none of these

7.

$$\frac{2}{3} \div \frac{7}{10}$$

Ⓐ 20 Ⓒ $\frac{9}{30}$

Ⓑ $\frac{20}{21}$ Ⓓ $\frac{14}{30}$

8.

$$3\frac{1}{2} \div 4\frac{7}{9} =$$

Ⓔ $1\frac{63}{86}$ Ⓖ 9

Ⓕ $\frac{63}{42}$ Ⓗ none of these

STOP

Mathematics: Adding Integers

Directions: Read each problem carefully. Fill in the correct answer circle.

Samples

A. $-10 + 5 =$

    Ⓐ -15   Ⓒ **-5**

    Ⓑ 15   Ⓓ 5

B. $-3 + -7 =$

    Ⓔ **-10**   Ⓖ 4

    Ⓕ 10   Ⓗ -4

---

1. $8 + -3 =$

    Ⓐ 5

    Ⓑ 11

    Ⓒ -5

    Ⓓ none of these

5. $-15 + 12 =$

    Ⓐ 3

    Ⓑ -3

    Ⓒ 27

    Ⓓ none of these

---

2. $-9 + -2 =$

    Ⓔ 11

    Ⓕ -11

    Ⓖ -9

    Ⓗ 9

6. $-5 + -9 =$

    Ⓔ 14

    Ⓕ 4

    Ⓖ -4

    Ⓗ -14

---

3. $2 + -7 =$

    Ⓐ 5

    Ⓑ 9

    Ⓒ -9

    Ⓓ -5

7. $14 + -7 =$

    Ⓐ 7

    Ⓑ -7

    Ⓒ 14

    Ⓓ none of these

---

4. $-6 + 7 =$

    Ⓔ 12

    Ⓕ -12

    Ⓖ 1

    Ⓗ -1

8. $8 + -12 =$

    Ⓔ 4

    Ⓕ 20

    Ⓖ -20

    Ⓗ none of these

STOP

Mathematics: Subtracting Integers

Directions: Read each problem carefully. Fill in the correct answer circle.

Samples

A. -5 – (-6) =

  Ⓐ -11   Ⓒ **1**

  Ⓑ -1   Ⓓ 0

B. - 6 – 8 =

  Ⓔ -1   Ⓖ 14

  Ⓕ 1   **Ⓗ -14**

---

1. -7 – (-3) =

  Ⓐ -4

  Ⓑ -10

  Ⓒ 10

  Ⓓ 4

5. -12 – (-9) =

  Ⓐ 3

  Ⓑ 21

  Ⓒ -3

  Ⓓ none of these

---

2. -12 – 8 =

  Ⓔ 20

  Ⓕ -4

  Ⓖ -20

  Ⓗ 4

6. -3 – 7 =

  Ⓔ -10

  Ⓕ 10

  Ⓖ 4

  Ⓗ -4

---

3. -9 – (-5) =

  Ⓐ 4

  Ⓑ -4

  Ⓒ 14

  Ⓓ -7

7. -7 – 7 =

  Ⓐ 14

  Ⓑ 0

  Ⓒ -0

  Ⓓ -14

---

4. -3 – 5 =

  Ⓔ 8

  Ⓕ -8

  Ⓖ 2

  Ⓗ -2

8. -10 – (-10) =

  Ⓔ -20

  Ⓕ 0

  Ⓖ 20

  Ⓗ -1

STOP

Mathematics: Multiplying Integers

Directions: Read each problem carefully. Fill in the correct answer circle.

Samples

A. 7 x (-5) =

Ⓐ **-35**   Ⓒ 12
Ⓑ 35   Ⓓ -12

B. -217 x (-54) =

Ⓔ **11,718**   Ⓖ 12,729
Ⓕ -11,758   Ⓗ -none of these

---

1. -57 x (-19) =

Ⓐ 1,083
Ⓑ 2,512
Ⓒ -1,083
Ⓓ none of these

5. -32 x (-27) =

Ⓐ 684
Ⓑ 864
Ⓒ 486
Ⓓ none of these

---

2. -73 x 56 =

Ⓔ 4,000
Ⓕ 4,251
Ⓖ -4,088
Ⓗ none of these

6. 54 x (-17) =

Ⓔ 918
Ⓕ -918
Ⓖ -819
Ⓗ 819

---

3. -47 x (-32) =

Ⓐ -1,504
Ⓑ 1,405
Ⓒ 1,504
Ⓓ none of these

7. 63 x (-12) =

Ⓐ 756
Ⓑ 765
Ⓒ 657
Ⓓ -756

---

4. -15 x 79 =

Ⓔ 1,185
Ⓕ 1,815
Ⓖ 1,518
Ⓗ none of these

8. -12 x (-13) =

Ⓔ 156
Ⓕ -156
Ⓖ 165
Ⓗ none of these

STOP

Mathematics: Dividing Integers

Directions: Read each problem carefully. Fill in the correct answer circle.

Samples

A. $-864 \div (-32) =$

- Ⓐ -27
- Ⓒ 72
- Ⓔ 81
- Ⓖ **-81**
- **Ⓑ 27**
- Ⓓ none of these
- Ⓕ 18
- Ⓗ -none of these

B. $-1215 \div 15 =$

---

1. $-884 \div (-52) =$
- Ⓐ -17
- Ⓑ 17
- Ⓒ -71
- Ⓓ 71

5. $(-504) \div -42 =$
- Ⓐ -12
- Ⓑ 21
- Ⓒ 12
- Ⓓ -21

2. $2976 \div (-32) =$
- Ⓔ 93
- Ⓕ -39
- Ⓖ -93
- Ⓗ none of these

6. $(-819) \div -13 =$
- Ⓔ 63
- Ⓕ -36
- Ⓖ 36
- Ⓗ -63

3. $858 \div (-66) =$
- Ⓐ -13
- Ⓑ 13
- Ⓒ 31
- Ⓓ -31

7. $299 \div (-13) =$
- Ⓐ 23
- Ⓑ 32
- Ⓒ -32
- Ⓓ none of these

4. $(-348) \div 12 =$
- Ⓔ -92
- Ⓕ -29
- Ⓖ 29
- Ⓗ 92

8. $522 \div (-9) =$
- Ⓔ -58
- Ⓕ 58
- Ⓖ -85
- Ⓗ 85

STOP

Mathematics: The Coordinate Plane

Directions: Use the coordinate plane to answer the questions.

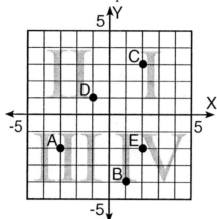

1. What are the coordinates of point A?
- Ⓐ (-3, -2)
- Ⓑ (3, 2)
- Ⓒ (-2, -3)
- Ⓓ (2, 3)

2. In what quadrant is point A located?
- Ⓔ II
- Ⓕ III
- Ⓖ I
- Ⓗ IV

3. What are the coordinates of point B?
- Ⓐ (1, 4)
- Ⓑ (4, 1)
- Ⓒ (1, -4)
- Ⓓ (-1, -4)

4. In what quadrant is point B located?
- Ⓔ I
- Ⓕ II
- Ⓖ III
- Ⓗ IV

5. What are the coordinates of point C?
- Ⓐ (-2, -3)
- Ⓑ (2, 3)
- Ⓒ (3, 2)
- Ⓓ (-3, -2)

6. What are the coordinates of point D?
- Ⓔ (1, 1)
- Ⓕ (-1, -1)
- Ⓖ (-1, 1)
- Ⓗ none of these

7. In what quadrant is point C located?
- Ⓐ II
- Ⓑ III
- Ⓒ IV
- Ⓓ I

8. What are the coordinates of point E?
- Ⓔ (2, -2)
- Ⓕ (2, 2)
- Ⓖ (-2, 2)
- Ⓗ (-2, -2)

9. In what quadrant is point E located?
- Ⓐ I
- Ⓑ IV
- Ⓒ II
- Ⓓ III

10. If a point were placed at coordinates (-2, 1) which point would it be nearest?
- Ⓔ C
- Ⓕ D
- Ⓖ B
- Ⓗ C

Mathematics: Ratio and Rate

Directions: Read each problem carefully. Fill in the correct answer circle.

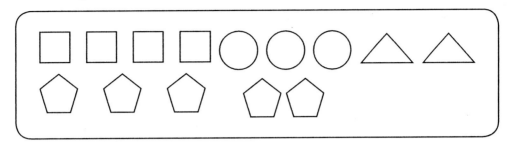

1. What is the ratio of triangles to circles?
   - (A) 2:3
   - (B) 3:2
   - (C) 4:2
   - (D) 2:4

2. What is the ratio of pentagons to squares?
   - (E) 2:3
   - (F) 3:2
   - (G) 5:4
   - (H) 3:3

3. Which ratio is equal to 5:7?
   - (A) 2:10
   - (B) 15:21
   - (C) 9:12
   - (D) 4:9

4. Which ratio is equal to 6:9?
   - (E) 3:10
   - (F) 2:10
   - (G) 0:2
   - (H) 24:36

5. Which ratio is equal to 18:36?
   - (A) 2:10
   - (B) 14:92
   - (C) 3:6
   - (D) 2:15

6. Mavis runs 3 miles in 39 minutes. What is Mavis's unit rate?
   - (E) 1 mile in 10 minutes
   - (F) 1 mile in 13 minutes
   - (G) 1 mile in 15 minutes
   - (H) 1 mile in 20 minutes

7. The speed limit is 45 miles per hour. If a person only drives the speed limit, how many miles will the person travel in 4 hours?
   - (A) 100 miles
   - (B) 180 miles
   - (C) 150 miles
   - (D) none of these

8. Sammy can swim 10 lengths of the pool in 20 minutes? What is Sammy's unit rate?
   - (E) 1 length in 1 minute
   - (F) 1 length in 1 ½ minutes
   - (G) 1 length in 3 minutes
   - (H) 1 length in 2 minutes

STOP

Mathematics: Proportions

Directions: Read each problem carefully. Fill in the correct answer circle.

Samples

A. Find the ratios that form a proportion.

Ⓐ $\frac{2}{5}$; $\frac{3}{6}$ Ⓒ $\frac{12}{24}$; $\frac{9}{12}$

Ⓑ $\frac{3}{5}$; $\frac{6}{10}$ Ⓓ $\frac{4}{5}$; $\frac{2}{10}$

B. Solve for x: $\frac{2}{10} = \frac{x}{15}$

Ⓔ x = 9   Ⓖ x = 3

Ⓕ x = 10   Ⓗ x = 7

---

1. Solve for x:

$\frac{5}{6} = \frac{x}{3}$

Ⓐ x = 2   Ⓒ x = 7

Ⓑ x = 2.5 Ⓓ none of these

5. Solve for m.

$\frac{26}{20} = \frac{39}{m}$

Ⓐ m = 30 Ⓒ m = 19

Ⓑ m = 28 Ⓓ none of these

---

2. Solve for p:

$\frac{8}{p} = \frac{6}{12}$

Ⓔ p = 11 Ⓖ p = 12

Ⓕ p = 13 Ⓗ p = 16

6. Solve for r:

$\frac{11}{33} = \frac{r}{120}$

Ⓔ r = 80 Ⓖ r = 0

Ⓕ r = 10 Ⓗ r = 40

---

3. Find the ratios that form a proportion.

Ⓐ $\frac{6}{3}$; $\frac{2}{5}$ Ⓒ $\frac{12}{9}$; $\frac{8}{6}$

Ⓑ $\frac{4}{8}$; $\frac{4}{9}$ Ⓓ none of these

7. Find the ratios that form a proportion.

Ⓐ $\frac{3}{9}$; $\frac{9}{0}$ Ⓒ $\frac{83}{29}$; $\frac{56}{12}$

Ⓑ $\frac{10}{34}$; $\frac{8}{19}$ Ⓓ $\frac{12}{6}$; $\frac{12}{6}$

---

4. Find the ratios that form a proportion.

Ⓔ $\frac{9}{1}$; $\frac{2}{30}$ Ⓖ $\frac{9}{18}$; $\frac{6}{12}$

Ⓕ $\frac{4}{19}$; $\frac{7}{10}$ Ⓗ $\frac{17}{23}$; $\frac{4}{5}$

8. Find the ratios that form a proportion.

Ⓔ $\frac{1}{9}$; $\frac{4}{36}$ Ⓖ $\frac{9}{12}$; $\frac{13}{9}$

Ⓕ $\frac{2}{27}$; $\frac{4}{10}$ Ⓗ none of these

STOP

Mathematics: Geometry

Directions: Read each problem carefully. Fill in the correct answer circle.

1. What are these lines called?

Ⓐ intersecting
Ⓑ parallel
Ⓒ perpendicular
Ⓓ crossing

2. What are these lines called?

Ⓔ parallel
Ⓕ perpendicular
Ⓖ crossing
Ⓗ segments

3. What kind of angle is this?

Ⓐ obtuse
Ⓑ acute
Ⓒ 30 degree
Ⓓ right

4. Which angle is less than 90 degrees?

Ⓔ obtuse
Ⓕ right
Ⓖ acute
Ⓗ sharp

5. What is the name of this angle?

Ⓐ <DEF
Ⓑ <EFD
Ⓒ <FED
Ⓓ Both A and C

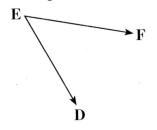

6. Two angles that add up to 180 degrees are called what?

Ⓔ supplementary
Ⓕ complementary
Ⓖ both of these
Ⓗ none of these

7. What kind of a triangle is this?

Ⓐ isosceles
Ⓑ scalene
Ⓒ equilateral
Ⓓ none of these

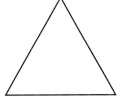

8. What defines a scalene triangle?

Ⓔ It has two sides of equal length.
Ⓕ It has three sides of equal length.
Ⓖ It is pointy
Ⓗ It has no sides of equal length.

9. What is this called?

Ⓐ ray line
Ⓑ line
Ⓒ line segment
Ⓓ end point

10. What kinds of lines are these?

Ⓔ adjacent
Ⓕ intersecting
Ⓖ infinity
Ⓗ perpendicular

Mathematics: Percents, Decimals, and Fractions

Directions: Read each problem carefully. Fill in the correct answer circle.

1. Convert 36% to a decimal.
- (A) 3.6
- (B) .36
- (C) .036
- (D) 36

2. Convert 2% to a fraction.
- (E) $\frac{20}{100}$
- (G) $\frac{200}{100}$
- (F) $\frac{2}{100}$
- (H) none of these

3. Convert 456% to a fraction.
- (A) $\frac{456}{1000}$
- (C) $4\frac{46}{100}$
- (B) $\frac{456}{100}$
- (D) none of these

4. Convert .27 to a percent.
- (E) 27%
- (F) 270%
- (G) 2.7%
- (H) none of these

5. Convert $\frac{72}{1000}$ to a decimal.
- (A) .72
- (B) 7.1
- (C) 72
- (D) .072

6. What is 50% of 66?
- (E) 30
- (F) 20
- (G) 33
- (H) 12

7. What is 37% of 23?
- (A) 8.51
- (B) 851
- (C) 1.85
- (D) none of these

8. What is 76% of 20?
- (E) 15.2
- (F) 152
- (G) 1.52
- (H) none of these

9. What is 83% of 34?
- (A) 2,822
- (B) 282
- (C) 222
- (D) 28.22

10. What is 75% of 50?
- (E) 375
- (F) 37.5
- (G) 37,500
- (H) none of these

Science: Weather I

Directions: Read each sentence or phrase carefully. Fill in the correct answer circle.

Sample

A. A person who studies the weather is called a what?
- (A) anthropologist
- (B) paleontologist
- (C) climatologist
- **(D) meteorologist**

---

1. What is a forecast?
   - (A) an attempt to predict the weather
   - (B) a weather pattern
   - (C) barometric pressure
   - (D) climate change

2. What causes air pressure?
   - (E) green house gases
   - (F) gas pushing against the surface of the earth
   - (G) moisture in the air
   - (H) all of these

3. What is created when air moves from high pressure to low pressure regions?
   - (A) rain
   - (B) snow
   - (C) hail
   - (D) wind

4. What might you experience on a very humid day?
   - (E) goose bumps
   - (F) chills
   - (G) perspiration
   - (H) frostbite

5. How does water vapor get into the air?
   - (A) condensation
   - (B) collection
   - (C) transpiration
   - (D) evaporation

6. If the relative humidity is 63 percent, how much more water vapor can the air hold?
   - (E) none
   - (F) 37 percent
   - (G) 126 percent
   - (H) 10 percent

7. Which types of clouds are made of ice crystals?
   - (A) cirrus
   - (B) stratus
   - (C) altocumulus
   - (D) all of these

8. What causes precipitation to fall from the sky?
   - (E) the heaviness of the clouds
   - (F) thunder and lightening
   - (G) gusty winds
   - (H) none of these

9. What is used to measure air pressure?
   - (A) a thermometer
   - (B) a necronmeter
   - (C) a weather gage
   - (D) a barometer

10. What does an anemometer measure?
    - (E) humidity
    - (F) wind speed
    - (G) hail size
    - (H) cloud temperatures

STOP

Science: Weather II

Directions: Read each sentence or phrase carefully. Fill in the correct answer circle.

Sample

A. A thermometer measures what?

Ⓐ **the temperature of the air**   Ⓒ wind speed

Ⓑ the moisture of the air   Ⓓ none of these

---

1. What can Doppler radar show?

   Ⓐ the dew point

   Ⓑ the direction in which a storm may be moving

   Ⓒ how much rain is contained within the storm system

   Ⓓ the length of the storm

2. Generally speaking, what size are air masses?

   Ⓔ very large

   Ⓕ very small

   Ⓖ about six square miles

   Ⓗ none of these

3. When a warm and a cold air mass meet, what is created?

   Ⓐ a front

   Ⓑ a back

   Ⓒ a pattern

   Ⓓ a jet stream

4. What causes the weather patterns in the U.S. to generally move from west to east?

   Ⓔ wind patterns

   Ⓕ the Pacific Ocean

   Ⓖ the size of the state of California

   Ⓗ the expanse of the Great Plains

5. What causes lightning?

   Ⓐ friction

   Ⓑ electrical charges in clouds

   Ⓒ thunder

   Ⓓ static electricity

6. What weather event is funnel-shaped?

   Ⓔ hurricane

   Ⓕ monsoon

   Ⓖ hailstorm

   Ⓗ tornado

7. What city was devastated by Hurricane Katrina?

   Ⓐ Dallas

   Ⓑ Orlando

   Ⓒ New Orleans

   Ⓓ all of these

8. Why shouldn't you talk on the phone during a thunder and lightning storm?

   Ⓔ lightning can travel through the phone

   Ⓕ you won't be able to hear the person to whom you are speaking

   Ⓖ emergency workers need the phone lines to be clear

   Ⓗ none of these

9. Hurricanes form around areas of what?

   Ⓐ low pressure

   Ⓑ high pressure

   Ⓒ high humidity

   Ⓓ cirrus clouds

10. A car, a telephone pole, a bike, a stop sign: which object is most likely to be struck by lightning?

   Ⓔ the bike

   Ⓕ the car

   Ⓖ the telephone pole

   Ⓗ the stop sign

Science: Geology I

Directions: Read each sentence or phrase carefully. Fill in the correct answer circle.

Sample
A. The outermost layer of the Earth is called what?

  Ⓐ the core   **Ⓒ the crust**

  Ⓑ the mantle   Ⓓ none of these

---

1. Where is the lithosphere located?

  Ⓐ in the core of the planet

  Ⓑ in the stratosphere of the planet

  Ⓒ in the ionosphere of the planet

  Ⓓ just beneath the crust of the planet

2. The lithosphere is comprised of what?

  Ⓔ rocks and boulders

  Ⓕ sandy soil

  Ⓖ large plates of rock

  Ⓗ none of these

3. What might you find at the place where two plates meet?

  Ⓐ a mountain

  Ⓑ a fault

  Ⓒ a canyon

  Ⓓ a plain

4. What causes the Earth's plates to move?

  Ⓔ the movement of molten rock in the mantle

  Ⓕ gravity

  Ⓖ pressure

  Ⓗ lithospheric turbulence

5. A fault boundary, a colliding boundary, and a spreading boundary are places where what meets?

  Ⓐ seismic waves

  Ⓑ underground mountain ranges

  Ⓒ plates

  Ⓓ all of these

6. During an earthquake, the focus is where what happens?

  Ⓔ where the rocks first move

  Ⓕ where the seismograph is located

  Ⓖ where the lava seeps through the ground

  Ⓗ none of these

7. What does a seismograph record?

  Ⓐ vibrations in the ground

  Ⓑ movements in the core

  Ⓒ movements in the mantle

  Ⓓ none of these

8. If an earthquake measures 7.3 on the Richter scale, what might you expect to see?

  Ⓔ very little damage

  Ⓕ moderate damage

  Ⓖ a major amount of damage

  Ⓗ all of these

9. What might you expect to find at colliding boundaries?

  Ⓐ a mountain

  Ⓑ a volcano

  Ⓒ a tsunami

  Ⓓ an earthquake

10. What can explode out of volcanoes?

  Ⓔ wind

  Ⓕ hail

  Ⓖ bacteria

  Ⓗ magma

(STOP)

Science: Geology II

Directions: Read each sentence or phrase carefully. Fill in the correct answer circle.

Sample
A. Where would you expect to find subsoil?
- Ⓐ above the topsoil
- Ⓒ under the mantle
- Ⓑ beneath the bedrock
- **Ⓓ below the topsoil**

---

1. What force causes rivers to flow downhill?
- Ⓐ inertia
- Ⓑ gravity
- Ⓒ friction
- Ⓓ push-pull forces

2. What is a drainage basin?
- Ⓔ a large river that drains into an ocean
- Ⓕ a river comprised of glacier waters
- Ⓖ the water from the land that drains into a river
- Ⓗ a land that drains into a river

3. What are sediments?
- Ⓐ soil and rock that's been eroded by a river
- Ⓑ water molecules
- Ⓒ a river delta
- Ⓓ all of these

4. The water in an aquifer is compromised of what?
- Ⓔ salt water
- Ⓕ condensed water
- Ⓖ water vapor
- Ⓗ groundwater

5. The top of an aquifer is called a what?
- Ⓐ wellspring
- Ⓑ water table
- Ⓒ geyser
- Ⓓ water slab

6. What is a moraine?
- Ⓔ a type of aquifer
- Ⓕ a type of ocean wave
- Ⓖ a type of stone deposited by a glacier
- Ⓗ none of these

7. Erosion can cause what?
- Ⓐ rocks to become soil
- Ⓑ river sediment
- Ⓒ shorelines
- Ⓓ all of these

8. Which of the following is characteristic of an index fossil?
- Ⓔ they are always large
- Ⓕ they are always small
- Ⓖ they are the remains of animals that existed for long periods of time
- Ⓗ they are the remains of animals that existed for short periods of time

9. Which is the oldest geologic period?
- Ⓐ Paleozoic
- Ⓑ Mesozoic
- Ⓒ Cenozoic
- Ⓓ Devonian

10. Limestone is a kind of what?
- Ⓔ shale
- Ⓕ sandstone
- Ⓖ coal
- Ⓗ sedimentary rock

Science: Astronomy I

Directions: Read each sentence or phrase carefully. Fill in the correct answer circle.

Sample

A. How long does it take Earth to make one rotation on its axis?

Ⓐ 365 days or 1 year   Ⓒ 1 month

Ⓑ 24 hours or 1 day   Ⓓ 1 lunar cycle

---

1. How is a planet's axis best described?
   - Ⓐ It is the planet's orbit.
   - Ⓑ An imaginary line on which a planet spins.
   - Ⓒ elliptical and orbital
   - Ⓓ none of these

2. Where does Earth's axis run?
   - Ⓔ around the equator
   - Ⓕ along the Prime Meridian
   - Ⓖ from the North Pole to the South Pole
   - Ⓗ along the lines of latitude

3. In which direction does the Earth rotate as viewed from the North Pole?
   - Ⓐ counterclockwise: from left to right
   - Ⓑ clockwise: from right to left
   - Ⓒ both A and B
   - Ⓓ none of these

4. Earth's axis causes what kind of change on Earth?
   - Ⓔ planetary rotation
   - Ⓕ lunar eclipses
   - Ⓖ solar eclipses
   - Ⓗ seasonal change

5. The longest and shortest days of the year are also known as what?
   - Ⓐ equinoxes
   - Ⓑ solstices
   - Ⓒ autumnal harvests
   - Ⓓ none of these

6. On what date do people in the Northern Hemisphere experience the summer solstice?
   - Ⓔ June 21st or 22nd
   - Ⓕ December 21st or 22nd
   - Ⓖ November 26th
   - Ⓗ January 1st

7. On what date do people in the Southern Hemisphere experience the summer solstice?
   - Ⓐ June 21st or 22nd
   - Ⓑ December 21st or 22nd
   - Ⓒ November 26th
   - Ⓓ January 1st

8. An equinox occurs how many times per year?
   - Ⓔ 10
   - Ⓕ 5
   - Ⓖ 7
   - Ⓗ 2

9. New, Gibbous, and First Quarter are what?
   - Ⓐ the moons of Saturn
   - Ⓑ the moons of Venus
   - Ⓒ phases of Earth's moon
   - Ⓓ types of telescopes

10. What determines how long a year is for our solar system's planets?
    - Ⓔ how quickly the planet spins on its axis
    - Ⓕ how severe the tilt of the axis is
    - Ⓖ proximity to its moon
    - Ⓗ how quickly the planet revolves around the sun

Science: Astronomy II

Directions: Read each sentence or phrase carefully. Fill in the correct answer circle.

Sample

A. How far away from Earth is our sun?

Ⓐ 200 million miles   **Ⓒ 93 million miles**

Ⓑ 200 billion miles   Ⓓ 150 million miles

---

1. About how long does it take for light from the sun to travel to Earth?

Ⓐ 15 minutes

Ⓑ 10 minutes

Ⓒ 1 year

Ⓓ 8 minutes

2. The sun's color is an indication of what?

Ⓔ its size

Ⓕ its temperature

Ⓖ its distance

Ⓗ its ultraviolet radiation

3. Of what is the sun comprised?

Ⓐ nitrogen

Ⓑ hydrogen and nitrogen

Ⓒ radiation

Ⓓ hydrogen and helium

4. What is the process by which hydrogen is combined with other elements to form helium?

Ⓔ fission

Ⓕ corona

Ⓖ fusion

Ⓗ none of these

5. This alignment of the sun, moon, and Earth would produce what?

Ⓐ solar eclipse

Ⓑ lunar eclipse

Ⓒ equinox

Ⓓ corona explosion

6. What causes a lunar eclipse?

Ⓔ the Earth passing between the sun and moon

Ⓕ the moon passing between the sun and Earth

Ⓖ the moon passing in the shadow of the Earth

Ⓗ none of these

7. Which of the following is characteristic of sunspots?

Ⓐ They are the hottest places on the sun.

Ⓑ It is where the hydrogen fusion takes place.

Ⓒ It is where the helium is created.

Ⓓ They are cooler than other places on the sun.

8. What can solar flares create?

Ⓔ auroras

Ⓕ eclipses

Ⓖ sunspots

Ⓗ all of these

9. Eruptions on the sun are called what?

Ⓐ aurora

Ⓑ corona

Ⓒ solar flares

Ⓓ none of these

10. What part of the sun can you see during a solar eclipse?

Ⓔ sun spots

Ⓕ corona

Ⓖ fusion creation

Ⓗ all of these

STOP

Science: Astronomy III

Directions: Read each sentence or phrase carefully. Fill in the correct answer circle.

> ## Sample
> **A.** The name of the galaxy in which we live is what?
>
> Ⓐ **Milky Way** Ⓒ Andromeda
>
> Ⓑ Alpha Centauri Ⓓ none of these

1. A galaxy can be defined as what?

Ⓐ a large solar system

Ⓑ a large collection of stars

Ⓒ a large system of stars, planets, moons, gases, and dust

Ⓓ none of these

2. What type of galaxy is the Milky Way?

Ⓔ elliptical

Ⓕ spiral

Ⓖ irregular

Ⓗ orbital

3. Which kind of galaxies are most prevalent?

Ⓐ elliptical

Ⓑ spiral

Ⓒ oval

Ⓓ irregular

4. The centers of distant, developing galaxies are called what?

Ⓔ black holes

Ⓕ dwarfs

Ⓖ quasars

Ⓗ pulsars

5. Which of the following colors can a star not be?

Ⓐ red

Ⓑ indigo

Ⓒ yellow

Ⓓ white

6. Where are stars created?

Ⓔ inside black holes

Ⓕ inside quasars

Ⓖ inside nebulas

Ⓗ none of these

7. What force is essential in the creation of new stars?

Ⓐ gravity

Ⓑ inertia

Ⓒ friction

Ⓓ fission

8. An exploding star is called a what?

Ⓔ neutron star

Ⓕ red giant

Ⓖ supernova

Ⓗ super-giant

9. What cannot escape a black hole?

Ⓐ hydrogen

Ⓑ light

Ⓒ oxygen

Ⓓ cosmic dust

10. If the color of an object in the universe shifts toward red it means what?

Ⓔ It is moving closer to us.

Ⓕ It is moving at the speed of light.

Ⓖ It is moving away from us.

Ⓗ It is stationary.

STOP

Science: Biology I

Directions: Read each sentence or phrase carefully. Fill in the correct answer circle.

Sample

A. Organisms that share characteristics are called what?

(A) types   (C) **species**

(B) families   (D) none of these

---

1. What is considered to be the basic building unit of all living things?
   - (A) nucleus
   - (B) cell
   - (C) DNA
   - (D) none of these

2. What acts as the kind of brain of a single cell?
   - (E) the cell membrane
   - (F) the chromosome
   - (G) the nucleus
   - (H) none of these

3. Where is the cytoplasm located?
   - (A) outside of the cell membrane
   - (B) inside the nucleus
   - (C) inside the chromosomes
   - (D) between the cell membrane and the nucleus

4. Mitochondria is a kind of what?
   - (E) cell
   - (F) organelle
   - (G) vacuole
   - (H) none of these

5. What is the function of the vacuole?
   - (A) combining proteins
   - (B) transporting materials
   - (C) storing materials
   - (D) energy production

6. Chloroplasts can be found in which of the following?
   - (E) plants only
   - (F) animals only
   - (G) both plants and animals
   - (H) plants and microscopic organisms

7. What color is chlorophyll?
   - (A) green
   - (B) white
   - (C) orange
   - (D) brown

8. For what is chlorophyll used?
   - (E) cell renewal
   - (F) food production
   - (G) waste removal
   - (H) none of these

9. The process by which plants make food is called what?
   - (A) osmosis
   - (B) photocytoplasm
   - (C) photosynthesis
   - (D) photomalange

10. Plant and animal cells both have what?
    - (E) ribosomes
    - (F) membranes
    - (G) chlorophyll
    - (H) all of these

STOP

Science: Biology II

Directions: Read each sentence or phrase carefully. Fill in the correct answer circle.

Sample

   A. Cell division occurs

    Ⓐ during mitosis   **Ⓒ after mitosis**

    Ⓑ before mitosis   Ⓓ none of the above

---

1. Where are chromosomes located?

  Ⓐ in the membrane

  Ⓑ in the nucleus

  Ⓒ in the platelets

  Ⓓ none of these

2. What occurs during mitosis?

  Ⓔ the cell membranes collapse

  Ⓕ parent cells die off

  Ⓖ DNA is formed

  Ⓗ identical nuclei are produced by a cell

3. What is the function of red blood cells?

  Ⓐ They stop bleeding.

  Ⓑ They carry oxygen.

  Ⓒ They protect against disease.

  Ⓓ They remove carbon monoxide.

4. How many cells are involved in asexual reproduction?

  Ⓔ one

  Ⓕ two

  Ⓖ seven

  Ⓗ none

5. How are sex cells formed?

  Ⓐ mitosis

  Ⓑ asexual reproduction

  Ⓒ meiosis

  Ⓓ none of these

6. What joins during fertilization?

  Ⓔ a zygote

  Ⓕ an egg cell and a sperm cell

  Ⓖ chromosomes

  Ⓗ DNA

7. During sexual reproduction, all living things begin as

  Ⓐ a single cell.

  Ⓑ a male and female cell.

  Ⓒ many cells.

  Ⓓ none of these

8. A zygote is

  Ⓔ a synonym for sexual reproduction.

  Ⓕ a synonym for asexual reproduction.

  Ⓖ a small egg.

  Ⓗ the first cell formed after sexual reproduction.

9. Similar characteristics in living things are called

  Ⓐ traits.

  Ⓑ eggs.

  Ⓒ chromosomes.

  Ⓓ base pairs.

10. What specifically controls traits?

  Ⓔ zygotes

  Ⓕ DNA

  Ⓖ genes

  Ⓗ all of these

STOP

Science: Biology III

Directions: Read each sentence or phrase carefully. Fill in the correct answer circle.

Sample

A. The molecules that comprise DNA are called what?

- (A) **bases**
- (B) nucleic acids
- (C) mitochondrial pairs
- (D) none of the above

1. Which letters represent the bases?
- (A) A, B, C, D
- (B) Y, X, X, Y
- (C) A, T, G, C
- (D) W, X, Y, Z

2. GC is an example of a what?
- (E) faulty gene
- (F) eye color gene
- (G) base pair
- (H) none of these

3. A child having the same color eyes as his father is an example of what?
- (A) heredity
- (B) inheritance
- (C) gene dispersal
- (D) gene pool decay

4. A dog that possesses two dominant genes is called a what?
- (E) hybrid
- (F) mutation
- (G) purebred
- (H) none of these

5. A gene that stops the expression of another gene is called what?
- (A) mutated
- (B) retroactive
- (C) recessive
- (D) dominant

6. Changes that occur in DNA are
- (E) predictable.
- (F) random.
- (G) harmless.
- (H) none of these

7. Changes in DNA are called what?
- (A) hybrids
- (B) intercellular disturbance
- (C) mutations
- (D) none of these

8. A recessive gene is
- (E) a gene that is expressed.
- (F) a gene that is dormant.
- (G) a gene that is mutated.
- (H) a gene that is not expressed.

9. How many chromosomes do people inherit from their parents?
- (A) 23
- (B) 46
- (C) 110
- (D) It depends on the age of the parents during sexual reproduction.

10. How many chromosomes do people inherit from their fathers?
- (E) 46
- (F) 23
- (G) 90
- (H) none of these

STOP

Science: Biology IV

Directions: Read each sentence or phrase carefully. Fill in the correct answer circle.

Sample

A. Reproducing and taking in energy are examples of what?

   Ⓐ animals   **Ⓒ life processes**

   Ⓑ plants   Ⓓ none of the above

---

1. From where does a plant get its energy?
   Ⓐ photosynthesis
   Ⓑ the sun
   Ⓒ carbon dioxide
   Ⓓ none of these

2. From where does a horse get its energy?
   Ⓔ food
   Ⓕ air
   Ⓖ the sun
   Ⓗ none of these

3. Adaptations are
   Ⓐ learned.
   Ⓑ inherited.
   Ⓒ unchanging.
   Ⓓ all of these

4. Beneficial mutations in a species causes the species to
   Ⓔ change.
   Ⓕ evolve.
   Ⓖ regress.
   Ⓗ all of these

5. The webbed feet of a wading bird are called
   Ⓐ a mutation.
   Ⓑ a genetic malfunction.
   Ⓒ a structural adaptation.
   Ⓓ none of these

6. Natural selection means that
   Ⓔ poorly adapted animals tend to survive.
   Ⓕ poorly adapted animals select sick mates.
   Ⓖ well adapted animals tend to survive.
   Ⓗ all animals with some form of adaptations survive.

7. A person covering his or her ears as a result of a loud bang is called a what?
   Ⓐ response
   Ⓑ stimulus
   Ⓒ a responding stimulus
   Ⓓ none of these

8. A change in the environment that causes a reaction is called a what?
   Ⓔ response
   Ⓕ proaction
   Ⓖ stimuli
   Ⓗ stimulus

9. Which of the following is an example of a physiological adaptation?
   Ⓐ a snake's scales
   Ⓑ an eagle's talons
   Ⓒ a prehensile tail
   Ⓓ fat production in hibernating bears

10. What type of adaptation is migration?
    Ⓔ structural
    Ⓕ instinctual
    Ⓖ physiological
    Ⓗ behavioral

STOP

Directions: Read each sentence or phrase carefully. Fill in the correct answer circle.

Sample

A. An ecosystem
  - Ⓐ contains only living organisms.
  - Ⓒ is larger than a biome.
  - Ⓑ contains only nonliving elements.
  - **Ⓓ is all the living and nonliving things in a particular area.**

---

1. What might an herbivore eat?
   - Ⓐ eggs
   - Ⓑ cheese
   - Ⓒ grass
   - Ⓓ carrion

2. Human beings are mostly
   - Ⓔ herbivores.
   - Ⓕ carnivores.
   - Ⓖ omnivores.
   - Ⓗ none of these

3. Fungi are
   - Ⓐ producers.
   - Ⓑ decomposers.
   - Ⓒ composers.
   - Ⓓ plants.

4. Why are decomposers important to an ecosystem?
   - Ⓔ They eat trash.
   - Ⓕ They break down nutrients that can be released back into the environment.
   - Ⓖ The eat poisonous plants.
   - Ⓗ none of these

5. Food webs can show
   - Ⓐ how things in an ecosystem are related.
   - Ⓑ how ecosystems evolve.
   - Ⓒ how nutrients move in an ecosystem.
   - Ⓓ none of these

6. Where is the most energy concentrated in an energy pyramid?
   - Ⓔ at the top
   - Ⓕ at the bottom
   - Ⓖ in the middle
   - Ⓗ in the top third

7. What role do animals play in photosynthesis?
   - Ⓐ They exhale the oxygen that plants need to make food.
   - Ⓑ They inhale the oxygen that plants need to make food.
   - Ⓒ They exhale the carbon dioxide that plants need to make food.
   - Ⓓ They eat the leaves of the plants and activate the chlorophyll.

GO

8. What causes nitrogen and oxygen to combine?
- Ⓔ lightning
- Ⓕ a certain type of bacteria
- Ⓖ hydrogen
- Ⓗ both E and F

9. Limited resources in a ecosystem cause
- Ⓐ confusion.
- Ⓑ dispersal.
- Ⓒ conflict.
- Ⓓ competition.

10. Deserts and tropical rain forests are examples of
- Ⓔ biomes.
- Ⓕ communities.
- Ⓖ eco-areas.
- Ⓗ none of these

11. What might you find in the taiga?
- Ⓐ palm trees
- Ⓑ deciduous trees
- Ⓒ coniferous trees
- Ⓓ permafrost

12. What might you find on the tundra?
- Ⓔ polar bears
- Ⓕ grizzly bears
- Ⓖ koala bears
- Ⓗ anacondas

13. Deciduous trees
- Ⓐ are evergreens.
- Ⓑ are shrubs.
- Ⓒ lose their leaves.
- Ⓓ all of these

14. Why are tropical rain forests located near the equator?
- Ⓔ The equator is very dry.
- Ⓕ The equator receives about 12 hours of sunlight every day.
- Ⓖ It is a large area.
- Ⓗ none of these

15. What kind of water is found in an estuary?
- Ⓐ salt water
- Ⓑ glacier water
- Ⓒ flowing water
- Ⓓ both freshwater and saltwater

Physical Science: Light and Sound

Directions: Read each sentence or phrase carefully. Fill in the correct answer circle.

Sample

A. Photons are the main component of

   Ⓐ sound.   Ⓒ matter.

   Ⓑ **light.**   Ⓓ all of these

---

1. Frequency and amplitude are measures of

   Ⓐ currents.

   Ⓑ photons.

   Ⓒ reflections.

   Ⓓ waves.

2. The number of waves that pass a certain point in a particular amount of time is

   Ⓔ amplitude.

   Ⓕ frequency.

   Ⓖ transverse.

   Ⓗ none of these

3. How does light travel?

   Ⓐ in spirals

   Ⓑ in straight lines

   Ⓒ in transverse waves

   Ⓓ none of the above

4. A mirror with a center that curves toward an object is called a what?

   Ⓔ convex mirror

   Ⓕ concave mirror

   Ⓖ elongated mirror

   Ⓗ shortened mirror

5. What causes light to be refracted?

   Ⓐ reflected light

   Ⓑ concave lenses

   Ⓒ laser beams

   Ⓓ movement from one clear substance to another.

6. The point at which rays of light meet is called

   Ⓔ the point of reflection.

   Ⓕ the point of refraction.

   Ⓖ the focal point.

   Ⓗ none of these

7. What is the source of gamma rays?

   Ⓐ the solar system

   Ⓑ the Earth's core

   Ⓒ the sun

   Ⓓ none of these

GO

Physical Science: Light and Sound *(cont.)*

8. Which of the following are visible to the human eye?
- Ⓔ ultraviolet waves
- Ⓕ infrared weaves
- Ⓖ x-rays
- Ⓗ none of these

9. What can you see on the visible spectrum of light?
- Ⓐ light waves
- Ⓑ color
- Ⓒ electromagnetism
- Ⓓ all of these

10. If an object is opaque,
- Ⓔ light can't pass through it.
- Ⓕ light can pass through it.
- Ⓖ only white light can pass through it.
- Ⓗ only black light can pass through it.

11. What must be present for there to be sound?
- Ⓐ light
- Ⓑ air
- Ⓒ waves
- Ⓓ none of these

12. The shorter the wavelength the
- Ⓔ lower the pitch.
- Ⓕ faster the pitch.
- Ⓖ higher the pitch.
- Ⓗ slower the pitch.

13. What is the measure of the intensity in sound waves?
- Ⓐ decibels
- Ⓑ amplitude
- Ⓒ pitch
- Ⓓ tone

14. An echo is a sound wave which is
- Ⓔ refracted.
- Ⓕ reflected.
- Ⓖ buffered.
- Ⓗ none of these

15. When one object strikes another what is created?
- Ⓐ an energy wave
- Ⓑ a vibration
- Ⓒ a transverse wave
- Ⓓ none of the above

STOP

Physical Science: Heat

Directions: Read each sentence or phrase carefully. Fill in the correct answer circle.

Sample

A. How is heat produced?

(A) **energy moving from a warmer object to a cooler object** (C) the temperature

(B) energy moving from a cooler object to a warmer object (D) none of these

---

1. The energy of the particles that comprise matter is called
   - (A) heat.
   - (B) temperature.
   - (C) thermal energy.
   - (D) all of these

2. What does temperature measure?
   - (E) heat
   - (F) the motion of particles in matter
   - (G) friction in matter
   - (H) none of these

3. Five ounces of tomato soup versus ten ounces of tomato soup: which will take longer to boil?
   - (A) ten ounces
   - (B) five ounces
   - (C) they will take the same amount of time
   - (D) depends on the size and shape of the pan

4. What happens to molecules when they are heated?
   - (E) the contract
   - (F) they expand
   - (G) they explode
   - (H) they move slowly

5. Which expands the most when heated?
   - (A) liquids
   - (B) solids
   - (C) gases
   - (D) solutions

6. A backyard grill uses what form of thermal energy to cook food?
   - (E) convection
   - (F) conduction
   - (G) insulation
   - (H) radiation

7. Heated water flowing through pipes in a home is an example of
   - (A) conduction.
   - (B) absorption.
   - (C) convection.
   - (D) radiation.

8. When you warm your hands over a fire, the heat of the fire is being
   - (E) conducted.
   - (F) converted.
   - (G) radiated.
   - (H) distributed.

9. Why is plastic a good insulator?
   - (A) It quickens the transfer of heat.
   - (B) It expands when heated.
   - (C) It contracts when heated.
   - (D) It slows down the transfer of heat.

10. What kind of thermal energy can travel without matter?
    - (E) conduction
    - (F) convection
    - (G) absorption
    - (H) radiation

STOP

Science: Chemistry

Directions: Read each sentence or phrase carefully. Fill in the correct answer circle.

Sample

A. Liquids, gases, and solids are called

Ⓐ matters of state.

Ⓑ states of matter.

Ⓒ terrestrial substances.

Ⓓ none of these.

---

1. In a gas the molecules are
   Ⓐ close together.
   Ⓑ stacked on top of each other.
   Ⓒ far apart.
   Ⓓ frozen.

2. How do molecules in solids move?
   Ⓔ They can move past each other.
   Ⓕ They can only vibrate.
   Ⓖ They move in all directions.
   Ⓗ They do not move at all.

3. What causes changes in matter?
   Ⓐ energy
   Ⓑ inertia
   Ⓒ radiation
   Ⓓ temperature

4. When a gas condenses, it changes into a
   Ⓔ solid.
   Ⓕ liquid.
   Ⓖ hot gas.
   Ⓗ cold gas.

5. What is the difference between a mixture and a solution?
   Ⓐ In a mixture, the substances dissolve so they can no longer be seen.
   Ⓑ In a solution, you can still see the elements that were combined.
   Ⓒ There are only two ingredients in a mixture.
   Ⓓ none of these

6. The sugar that dissolves in water is called
   Ⓔ a mixture.
   Ⓕ a solvent.
   Ⓖ a solute.
   Ⓗ none of these

7. Which of the following statements is true?
   Ⓐ A dilute has more solute than solvent.
   Ⓑ A concentrate has more solvent than solute.
   Ⓒ A dilute and a concentrate have the same solute to solvent ratio.
   Ⓓ A dilute has less solute than solvent.

8. What will increase dissolution?
   Ⓔ cold
   Ⓕ heat
   Ⓖ stirring
   Ⓗ Both F and G

GO

9. What holds the elements in a compound together?
- Ⓐ magnetism
- Ⓑ a chemical bond
- Ⓒ an electrical charge
- Ⓓ none of these

10. Chemical reactions create
- Ⓔ chemical compounds.
- Ⓕ products.
- Ⓖ chemical elements.
- Ⓗ none of these

11. In an endothermic reaction,
- Ⓐ more energy is taken in than released.
- Ⓑ more energy is released than taken in.
- Ⓒ the amount of energy absorbed and released is equal.
- Ⓓ reactants collide.

12. H_2O is an example of a(n)
- Ⓔ element.
- Ⓕ solvent.
- Ⓖ formula.
- Ⓗ none of these

13. What does a chemical equation show?
- Ⓐ what happens during a chemical reaction
- Ⓑ the formulas of compounds
- Ⓒ how much energy is released during a chemical reaction
- Ⓓ none of these

14. What does the pH scale measure?
- Ⓔ solvents
- Ⓕ chemical compounds
- Ⓖ acids
- Ⓗ acids and bases

15. The lower a substance is on the pH scale,
- Ⓐ the stronger the base.
- Ⓑ the stronger the acid.
- Ⓒ the more neutral.
- Ⓓ none of these

16. If a substance changes color on the pH scale, it is called
- Ⓔ a base.
- Ⓕ an acid.
- Ⓖ an indicator.
- Ⓗ a solution.

STOP

Science: Force and Motion

Directions: Read each sentence or phrase carefully. Fill in the correct answer circle.

> ## Sample
> A. Which of the following is an example of a force?
>
> (A) pushing a shopping cart   (C) hitting a baseball
>
> (B) states of matter   **(D) all of these**

1. What force causes objects to fall back to Earth?
   (A) friction   (C) mass
   (B) inertia   (D) gravity

2. Mass is determined by how much _____ an object contains.
   (E) gravity   (G) matter
   (F) newtons   (H) force

3. Which of the following statements is true?
   (A) You would weigh the same on the moon as you do on the Earth.
   (B) You would weigh more on the moon than you do on the Earth.
   (C) You would weigh less on the moon that you do on the Earth.
   (D) none of these

4. If you lift a book over your head the force you exert is
   (E) less than the force of gravity.
   (F) greater than the force of gravity.
   (G) equal to the force of gravity.
   (H) five times greater than the force of gravity.

5. In order for there to be a winner in an arm wrestling competition,
   (A) the forces must be unbalanced.
   (B) the forces must be balanced.
   (C) the forces must be equal.
   (D) none of these

6. Relative motion relies upon the _____ of two objects.
   (E) contract
   (F) gravity
   (G) force
   (H) comparison

7. Speed equals
   (A) time divided by distance.
   (B) time multiplied by distance.
   (C) distance multiplied by time.
   (D) distance divided by time.

(GO)

Science: Force and Motion *(cont.)*

8. Instantaneous speed refers to
- Ⓔ the initial speed of an object.
- Ⓕ the end speed of an object.
- Ⓖ the speed of an object at any given point.
- Ⓗ none of there

9. Velccity measures
- Ⓐ speed and distance.
- Ⓑ speed and force.
- Ⓒ speed and mass.
- Ⓓ speed and direction.

10. The rate at which speed changes is called
- Ⓔ acceleration.
- Ⓕ velocity.
- Ⓖ instantaneous speed.
- Ⓗ all of these

11. Which of the following objects has the most inertia?
- Ⓐ a rubber band
- Ⓑ a baseball
- Ⓒ a car
- Ⓓ a tissue

12. The force which slows down a bowling ball being rolled down an alley is
- Ⓔ friction.
- Ⓕ inertia.
- Ⓖ gravity.
- Ⓗ push-pull.

13. In which direction will an object travel unless it is acted upon?
- Ⓐ circular
- Ⓑ elliptical
- Ⓒ zig-zag
- Ⓓ straight line

14. Mass multiplied by acceleration is the equation for
- Ⓔ force.
- Ⓕ velocity.
- Ⓖ speed.
- Ⓗ none of these

15. For every action there is an
- Ⓐ force of inertia.
- Ⓑ equal and opposite reaction.
- Ⓒ pull force.
- Ⓓ all of these

(STOP)

Science: Health and the Human Body I

Directions: Read each sentence or phrase carefully. Fill in the correct answer circle.

Sample

A. What is a neuron?

- Ⓐ **a nerve cell**
- Ⓑ a cardiac cell
- Ⓒ an abdominal cell
- Ⓓ all of these

---

1. The hypothalamus controls
   - Ⓐ height.
   - Ⓑ weight.
   - Ⓒ body temperature.
   - Ⓓ intelligence.

2. What does the brain stem control?
   - Ⓔ breathing
   - Ⓕ reasoning
   - Ⓖ humor
   - Ⓗ emotions

3. Damage to the cerebellum might impair
   - Ⓐ language.
   - Ⓑ sight.
   - Ⓒ speech.
   - Ⓓ balance.

4. The peripheral nervous system
   - Ⓔ connects the brain and the spinal chord.
   - Ⓕ connects the nervous system to the rest of your body.
   - Ⓖ connects the cerebrum and the brain stem.
   - Ⓗ connects a sensory receptor to a motor neuron.

5. What carries information from the central nervous system to your biceps?
   - Ⓐ sensory neurons
   - Ⓑ muscle neurons
   - Ⓒ motor neurons
   - Ⓓ bicep neurons

6. Ducking, coughing, and sneezing are examples of what?
   - Ⓔ autoneuronic response
   - Ⓕ reflexes
   - Ⓖ axon movements
   - Ⓗ none of these

7. What is the role of the dendrite in the central nervous system?
   - Ⓐ They send messages between neurons.
   - Ⓑ They fill the gap between the synapse and the axon.
   - Ⓒ They collect information from neurons.
   - Ⓓ They monitor reflexive movements.

GO

Science: Health and Human Body *(cont.)*

8. In what part of the body would you find the retina?
- Ⓔ eyes
- Ⓕ ears
- Ⓖ mid-brain
- Ⓗ tongue

9. What system in the body controls hormones?
- Ⓐ reproductive
- Ⓑ digestive
- Ⓒ endocrine
- Ⓓ cardiovascular

10. Glands release
- Ⓔ hormones.
- Ⓕ neurons.
- Ⓖ bile.
- Ⓗ gastric acid.

11. Where is the pituitary gland located?
- Ⓐ the stomach
- Ⓑ the armpit
- Ⓒ the lower abdomen
- Ⓓ the brain

12. Which of the following is a stimulant?
- Ⓔ coffee
- Ⓕ cola
- Ⓖ nicotine
- Ⓗ all of these

13. Inhalants like glue can cause
- Ⓐ death.
- Ⓑ brain damage.
- Ⓒ vomiting.
- Ⓓ all of these

14. Long-term effects of marijuana can be
- Ⓔ diseases of the lungs.
- Ⓕ head and neck cancer.
- Ⓖ mental addiction.
- Ⓗ all of these

15. Cirrhosis is a fatal disease caused by
- Ⓐ stimulants.
- Ⓑ depressants.
- Ⓒ alcohol abuse.
- Ⓓ none of these

STOP

Social Studies: Prehistory

Directions: Read each sentence or phrase carefully. Fill in the correct answer circle.

Sample

A. Prehistory refers to the time before what?
- Ⓐ homo sapiens
- Ⓑ the industrial age
- **Ⓒ written language**
- Ⓓ the Roman Empire

---

1. An artifact is
- Ⓐ a fossil.
- Ⓑ something people made long ago.
- Ⓒ amber.
- Ⓓ none of these

2. The study of artifacts is called
- Ⓔ anthropology.
- Ⓕ paleontology.
- Ⓖ artifactology.
- Ⓗ archeology.

3. How long ago did the first humans live in Africa?
- Ⓐ about 10 million years ago
- Ⓑ about 3 ½ million years ago
- Ⓒ about 1 million years ago
- Ⓓ about 300,000 years ago

4. The process of people moving from place to place is called
- Ⓔ migration.
- Ⓕ dispersal.
- Ⓖ Diaspora.
- Ⓗ removal.

5. About how long ago did the Clovis people live in North America?
- Ⓐ 15,000 years ago
- Ⓑ 5,000 years ago
- Ⓒ 100,000 years ago
- Ⓓ 11,000 years ago

6. The land bridge over which people migrated from Asia to North America is called
- Ⓔ Pangaea.
- Ⓕ Outer Mongolia.
- Ⓖ Beringia.
- Ⓗ Bering Canal.

7. Why is the Topper site in South Carolina significant?
- Ⓐ It proved the existence of people in North America before the Clovis.
- Ⓑ It proved that the Clovis were the oldest people in North America.
- Ⓒ It was the first time a new archeological technology was used.
- Ⓓ none of these

GO

8. Why is the Stone Age called the Stone Age?

Ⓔ Because people fought wars with stones.

Ⓕ Because people made fire with stones.

Ⓖ Because people farmed with stones.

Ⓗ Because people made tools from stones.

9. What signaled the end of the Old Stone Age?

Ⓐ another Ice Age

Ⓑ the discovery of metals

Ⓒ the discovery of horses

Ⓓ the discovery of fire

10. Which animals were the first to be domesticated?

Ⓔ dogs

Ⓕ sheep

Ⓖ donkeys

Ⓗ roosters

11. Early farming contributed to the rise of

Ⓐ villages.

Ⓑ obesity.

Ⓒ toolmaking.

Ⓓ none of these

12. Nomads are

Ⓔ domesticated sheep.

Ⓕ domesticated goats.

Ⓖ types of stone tools.

Ⓗ people who move from place to place.

13. What type of metal was used during the New Stone Age?

Ⓐ copper

Ⓑ iron

Ⓒ bronze

Ⓓ tin

14. What technique is used to date the remains of animals, plants, and people?

Ⓔ DNA

Ⓕ archeobiology

Ⓖ carbon dating

Ⓗ none of these

15. Which of the following statements is false?

Ⓐ Technology changed rapidly during the Old Stone Age.

Ⓑ Technology changed slowly during the Old Stone Age.

Ⓒ Prehistoric technology varied greatly depending on which continent the people lived.

Ⓓ Prehistoric people did not have technology.

STOP

Social Studies: Early Civilizations

Directions: Read each sentence or phrase carefully. Fill in the correct answer circle.

Sample

A. An artisan might make

  Ⓐ houses   Ⓑ **pots**   Ⓒ bread   Ⓓ none of these

---

1. Why was the Fertile Crescent such an ideal location for early civilizations?
   - Ⓐ It kept warring tribes separated.
   - Ⓑ It was between two rivers.
   - Ⓒ It was mountainous.
   - Ⓓ There were large stores of copper in the mountains.

2. Which two rivers are located along the Fertile Crescent?
   - Ⓔ the Nile and the Ganges
   - Ⓕ the Amazon and the Yangtze
   - Ⓖ the Tigris and Euphrates
   - Ⓗ the Red Sea and the Dead Sea

3. Another name for the Fertile Crescent is
   - Ⓐ Egypt.
   - Ⓑ Umma.
   - Ⓒ Lagash.
   - Ⓓ Mesopotamia.

4. Ur, Uruk, and Nippur are names of
   - Ⓔ Mesopotamian city-states.
   - Ⓕ Mesopotamian scholars.
   - Ⓖ type of dwellings.
   - Ⓗ none of these

5. Polytheism is
   - Ⓐ the religious practice of worshipping one god.
   - Ⓑ the religious practice of worshipping animals.
   - Ⓒ the religious practice of worshipping many gods.
   - Ⓓ the religious practice of worshipping oracles.

6. Cuneiform is a type of
   - Ⓔ writing.
   - Ⓕ temple.
   - Ⓖ food.
   - Ⓗ tribal leader.

7. The empire of Hammurabi was
   - Ⓐ Asyria.
   - Ⓑ Sumeria.
   - Ⓒ Babylon.
   - Ⓓ none of these

8. The religious practice of worshipping one god is called
   - Ⓔ polytheism.
   - Ⓕ atheism.
   - Ⓖ Christianity.
   - Ⓗ monotheism.

9. About how long ago did the wheel appear in early civilizations?
   - Ⓐ 10,000 years ago
   - Ⓑ 5,000 years ago
   - Ⓒ 2,000 years ago
   - Ⓓ 1,000 years ago

10. Assyria was located in
    - Ⓔ the northern part of Babylonia.
    - Ⓕ the southern part of Babylonia.
    - Ⓖ the eastern part of Babylonia.
    - Ⓗ the western part of Babylonia.

STOP

Social Studies: Ancient Civilizations

Directions: Read each sentence or phrase carefully. Fill in the correct answer circle.

Sample

A. Through what African country does the Nile River run?

  Ⓐ Morocco   **Ⓑ Egypt**   Ⓒ Memphis   Ⓓ none of these

---

1. For what was papyrus used?

  Ⓐ to make tools

  Ⓑ to make pottery

  Ⓒ to make clothing

  Ⓓ to make paper

2. Why was the Nile River so critical to the development of the Egyptian Empire?

  Ⓔ Because it was full of fish.

  Ⓕ Because the Egyptians prayed to the water gods.

  Ⓖ Because there is very little rain and the river was used to irrigate crops.

  Ⓗ Because it protected the Egyptians from their enemies.

3. Old, Middle, and New Kingdoms are

  Ⓐ divisions in ancient Egyptian history.

  Ⓑ the names of various African kingdoms.

  Ⓒ the names of ancient books about Egypt.

  Ⓓ none of these

4. What is the significance of the Rosetta Stone?

  Ⓔ It helped archeologists learn about Egyptian tools.

  Ⓕ It was the oldest stone tool ever discovered.

  Ⓖ It helped archeologists translate hieroglyphics.

  Ⓗ none of these

5. Where is Egypt's largest pyramid located?

  Ⓐ Memphis

  Ⓑ Giza

  Ⓒ Cairo

  Ⓓ Fez

6. Pyramids were often used

  Ⓔ as tombs.

  Ⓕ as churches.

  Ⓖ as marketplaces.

  Ⓗ none of these

7. One of Africa's most ancient civilizations was called

  Ⓐ Nubia.

  Ⓑ Assyria.

  Ⓒ Lower Egypt.

  Ⓓ none of these

8. An Egyptian ruler was called a

  Ⓔ chief.

  Ⓕ warlord.

  Ⓖ pharoah.

  Ⓗ none of these

9. During what era did an Egyptian middle class emerge?

  Ⓐ the Old Kingdom

  Ⓑ the New Kingdom

  Ⓒ the Middle Kingdom

  Ⓓ none of these

10. Which of the following statements is false?

  Ⓔ The Nubians did not have a written language.

  Ⓕ The Nubians built irrigation channels.

  Ⓖ Nubia was located near what we call the Sudan today.

  Ⓗ all of these

(GO)

11. Which river flows through the North China Plain?
    - Ⓐ the Yellow River
    - Ⓑ the Yangtze River
    - Ⓒ the Nile River
    - Ⓓ the Huang River

12. A pictograph is
    - Ⓔ a type of portrait.
    - Ⓕ a type of written language.
    - Ⓖ a type of tool used for farming.
    - Ⓗ none of these

13. The Xia period in China's history refers to
    - Ⓐ prehistoric times.
    - Ⓑ the copper age.
    - Ⓒ the bronze age.
    - Ⓓ the iron age.

14. Which was the first Chinese Dynasty?
    - Ⓔ Ming
    - Ⓕ Zhou
    - Ⓖ Han
    - Ⓗ Shang

15. Which was China's longest dynasty?
    - Ⓐ Shang
    - Ⓑ Zhou
    - Ⓒ Qin
    - Ⓓ Yang

16. What did the Silk Road connect?
    - Ⓔ China to Japan
    - Ⓕ China to Africa
    - Ⓖ China to the Roman Empire
    - Ⓗ China to the Fertile Crescent

17. Where is the Indus River Valley located?
    - Ⓐ China
    - Ⓑ India
    - Ⓒ Africa
    - Ⓓ South America

18. What is Sanskrit?
    - Ⓔ a language
    - Ⓕ a religion
    - Ⓖ a form of irrigation
    - Ⓗ an Indian leader

19. Who is considered to be the founder of the Persian Empire?
    - Ⓐ Darius I
    - Ⓑ Ashoka
    - Ⓒ Cyrus II
    - Ⓓ Gilgamesh

20. Hinduism and Buddhism are religions that both believe in
    - Ⓔ reincarnation.
    - Ⓕ animal sacrifice.
    - Ⓖ The Ten Commandments.
    - Ⓗ Ra.

STOP

Social Studies: Ancient Greece

Directions: Read each sentence or phrase carefully. Fill in the correct answer circle.

Sample
A. On what peninsula is Greece located?

  Ⓐ **Balkan**   Ⓒ Kola

  Ⓑ Iberian   Ⓓ Asia Minor

---

1. On what island was the Minoan civilization located?

   Ⓐ Dokos

   Ⓑ Poros

   Ⓒ Crete

   Ⓓ Elba

2. What are myths usually about?

   Ⓔ wars

   Ⓕ feats of strength

   Ⓖ gods and goddesses

   Ⓗ climatic events

3. Who is believed to have written the epic poem "The Odyssey"?

   Ⓐ Ulysses

   Ⓑ Virgil

   Ⓒ Euripides

   Ⓓ Homer

4. How does an Athenian democracy differ from a modern democracy?

   Ⓔ A modern democracy is more efficient.

   Ⓕ An Athenian democracy still had a king.

   Ⓖ An Athenian democracy excluded women from the political process.

   Ⓗ none of these

5. With whom did the Athenians join with to defeat the Persian Empire?

   Ⓐ the Egyptians

   Ⓑ the Nubians

   Ⓒ the Spartans

   Ⓓ the Mongols

(GO)

Social Studies: Ancient Greece (cont.)

6. The agreement between Greek city-states was called
- Ⓔ the Delian League.
- Ⓕ the Great Compromise.
- Ⓖ the Delian Alliance.
- Ⓗ The Spartan-Athenian Coalition.

7. The war between Athens and Sparta was called
- Ⓐ the Trojan War.
- Ⓑ the Macedonian War.
- Ⓒ the Peloponnesian War.
- Ⓓ None of these

8. Socrates was a proponent of
- Ⓔ beauty.
- Ⓕ logic.
- Ⓖ poetic understanding.
- Ⓗ idealism.

9. What city-state defeated the Spartans?
- Ⓐ Athens
- Ⓑ Macedonia
- Ⓒ Cairo
- Ⓓ Thebes

10. Who was the king of Macedonia?
- Ⓔ Plato
- Ⓕ Hippocrates
- Ⓖ Alexander
- Ⓗ Euclid

11. The Hellenistic Age was a result of
- Ⓐ Alexander's conquest of the Persians.
- Ⓑ the Persian conquest of Macedonia.
- Ⓒ the Egyptian conquest of the Nubians.
- Ⓓ the Athenian conquest of Sparta.

12. Euclid is associated with what branch of mathematics?
- Ⓔ trigonometry
- Ⓕ calculus
- Ⓖ algebra
- Ⓗ geometry

13. What famous structure was built at the port at Alexandria?
- Ⓐ a library
- Ⓑ a pyramid
- Ⓒ a lighthouse
- Ⓓ the tomb of Alexander

STOP

Social Studies: Ancient Rome

Directions: Read each sentence or phrase carefully. Fill in the correct answer circle.

Sample

A. Along what river is Rome located?
- Ⓐ Adriatic
- Ⓑ Mediterranean
- Ⓒ **Tiber**
- Ⓓ none of these

1. Which people lived to the north of Rome?
- Ⓐ the Etruscans
- Ⓑ the Gauls
- Ⓒ the Barbarians
- Ⓓ the Saxons

2. Who were the patricians?
- Ⓔ the poorest people in Roman society
- Ⓕ the educated class in Roman society
- Ⓖ the richest people in Roman society
- Ⓗ the soldiers in Roman society

3. What was the role of the tribunes?
- Ⓐ They maintained order in the Roman Senate.
- Ⓑ The represented the plebeians in the Roman Senate.
- Ⓒ The represented the patricians in the Roman Senate.
- Ⓓ none of these

4. During the Punic Wars Rome battled
- Ⓔ Greece.
- Ⓕ the Etruscans.
- Ⓖ Carthage.
- Ⓗ Troy.

5. Why was Julius Caesar assassinated?
- Ⓐ He wanted to free the slaves.
- Ⓑ People feared he would dismantle the Republic.
- Ⓒ He was caught taking bribes from Patricians.
- Ⓓ none of these

GO

Social Studies: Ancient Rome *(cont.)*

6. To what does the Pax Romana refer?

   Ⓔ A long period of peace in the Roman Empire.

   Ⓕ An alliance of city-states.

   Ⓖ A period of great turmoil.

   Ⓗ A slave rebellion.

7. Which structure was a venue for Roman entertainment?

   Ⓐ the Acropolis

   Ⓑ Mount Olympus

   Ⓒ the Colosseum

   Ⓓ all of these

8. Which of the following was considered a great Roman Emperor?

   Ⓔ Caligula

   Ⓕ Nero

   Ⓖ Marcus Aurelius

   Ⓗ none of these

9. Why did Emperor Diocletian divide the Roman Empire?

   Ⓐ to avert a war

   Ⓑ to make governing easier and more effective

   Ⓒ to increase tax revenue

   Ⓓ to name a relative co-emperor

10. Which Roman Emperor reunited the empire?

   Ⓔ Claudius

   Ⓕ Julius Caesar

   Ⓖ Constantine

   Ⓗ none of these

11. What was Byzantium?

   Ⓐ a city-state

   Ⓑ the capital of the Roman Empire after reunification

   Ⓒ the capital of the western part of the Roman Empire

   Ⓓ none of these

12. What significant event occurred after the death of Constantine?

   Ⓔ the rise of Christianity

   Ⓕ the rise of Islam

   Ⓖ the second split of the Roman Empire

   Ⓗ the beginning of the Punic Wars

13. What caused the emergence of the Roman Catholic Church and the Byzantine Orthodox Church?

   Ⓐ disagreements over financial matters

   Ⓑ disagreements over Roman Emperors

   Ⓒ disagreements over the location of the seat of the church

   Ⓓ disagreements over who heads the church

STOP

Social Studies: The Middle Ages

Directions: Read each sentence or phrase carefully. Fill in the correct answer circle.

Sample

A. The Byzantine Empire is most closely associated with what other empire?

Ⓐ Egyptian   **Ⓒ Roman**

Ⓑ Greek   Ⓓ none of these

---

1. What was the capital of the Byzantine Empire?

Ⓐ Rome

Ⓑ Thebes

Ⓒ Constantinople

Ⓓ Cairo

2. What is a hippodrome?

Ⓔ a type of chariot

Ⓕ a type of arch

Ⓖ an ancient sport

Ⓗ a large arena

3. The Justinian Code

Ⓐ organized the laws of the Romans.

Ⓑ was the precursor of the Magna Carta.

Ⓒ was the code of the Roman soldier.

Ⓓ none of these

4. What kind of information was contained in the Domesday Book?

Ⓔ information about population

Ⓕ information about the solar system

Ⓖ information about witchcraft

Ⓗ information about architecture

5. Which of the following areas came under the rule of Charlemagne?

Ⓐ France

Ⓑ Spain

Ⓒ England

Ⓓ Russia

(GO)

6. William the Conqueror was a(n)
   - Ⓔ Saxon.
   - Ⓕ Frankish.
   - Ⓖ Norman.
   - Ⓗ Anglo.

7. What was the significance of the Magna Carta?
   - Ⓐ It consolidated power in the hands of the nobles.
   - Ⓑ It divided the church into factions.
   - Ⓒ It marked the end of the Norman Conquest.
   - Ⓓ It limited the power of the king.

8. The predominant social structure of the middle ages was
   - Ⓔ constructionism.
   - Ⓕ industrialism.
   - Ⓖ feudalism.
   - Ⓗ monarchism.

9. Who abided by the code of chivalry?
   - Ⓐ knights
   - Ⓑ monks
   - Ⓒ serfs
   - Ⓓ nobles

10. What were the advantages of belonging to a guild?
    - Ⓔ You had the protection of a knight.
    - Ⓕ You were able to own your own lands.
    - Ⓖ The guild provided a pension after your death.
    - Ⓗ The guild limited competition.

11. What was the mission of the Crusades?
    - Ⓐ to spread Christianity
    - Ⓑ to establish new trade routes to the Middle East
    - Ⓒ to retake control of Palestine
    - Ⓓ to conquer Persia

12. What was the Silk Road?
    - Ⓔ a land route to and from China
    - Ⓕ the route the Crusaders took to reach Palestine
    - Ⓖ the road to the palace of Genghis Khan
    - Ⓗ the name of Marco Polo's biography

13. What two animals were significant in the transmission of the plague?
    - Ⓐ rats and snakes
    - Ⓑ rats and fleas
    - Ⓒ fleas and dogs
    - Ⓓ rats and mosquitoes

STOP

Social Studies: Mesoamerica

Directions: Read each sentence or phrase carefully. Fill in the correct answer circle.

Sample

A. Which is considered the first great civilization of Mesoamerica?

  Ⓐ Maya   Ⓒ **Olmec**

  Ⓑ Inca   Ⓓ Aztec

1. Olmec government was a
  Ⓐ theocracy.
  Ⓑ democracy.
  Ⓒ oligarchy.
  Ⓓ dictatorship.

2. What other Mesoamerican civilizations did the Olmec influence?
  Ⓔ Maya
  Ⓕ Aztec
  Ⓖ Inca
  Ⓗ Both E and F

3. What does an aqueduct carry?
  Ⓐ grain
  Ⓑ mules
  Ⓒ water
  Ⓓ none of these

4. What is a codex?
  Ⓔ a type of Mayan farming technique
  Ⓕ the name of a Mayan god
  Ⓖ the name of a Mayan village
  Ⓗ a kind of Mayan book

5. What caused the decline of the Mayan civilization?
  Ⓐ disease
  Ⓑ political turmoil
  Ⓒ drought
  Ⓓ no one really knows for sure

6. Tenochtitlan is associated with what civilization?
  Ⓔ Aztec
  Ⓕ Maya
  Ⓖ Inca
  Ⓗ Olmec

7. Chinampas are
  Ⓐ man-made canals.
  Ⓑ a type of bread made by the Aztecs.
  Ⓒ man-made islands.
  Ⓓ a Maya game using a rubber ball.

8. Montezuma I and Montezuma II were
  Ⓔ Olmec warriors.
  Ⓕ Aztec rulers.
  Ⓖ Inca scholars.
  Ⓗ Aztec gods.

9. What did the Aztecs sacrifice to their gods?
  Ⓐ maize
  Ⓑ goats and sheep
  Ⓒ people
  Ⓓ bananas

10. Who played an important role in the demise of the Aztec Empire?
  Ⓔ Columbus
  Ⓕ Coronado
  Ⓖ De Soto
  Ⓗ Cortés

STOP

Social Studies: Native People of North and South America

Directions: Read each sentence or phrase carefully. Fill in the correct answer circle.

Sample

A. The Pantanal is
- Ⓐ a desert.
- Ⓑ a mountain peak in the Andes.
- Ⓒ a river in Canada.
- **Ⓓ a large wetland.**

---

1. What do the Inca, Chavin, and Mochia have in common?
- Ⓐ They are all North American tribes.
- Ⓑ They were all mound builders.
- Ⓒ They all lived in the area now called Peru.
- Ⓓ They were all hunters and gathers.

2. What city was the Inca capital?
- Ⓔ Cuzco
- Ⓕ Machu Picchu
- Ⓖ Snaketown
- Ⓗ none of these

3. What is often referred to as the *backbone* of North America?
- Ⓐ the Appalachian Mountains
- Ⓑ the Canadian Shield
- Ⓒ the Grand Canyon
- Ⓓ the Rocky Mountains

4. From what are pueblos made?
- Ⓔ stones
- Ⓕ adobe bricks
- Ⓖ mud and stars
- Ⓗ animal skins

5. Why did early North American people build mounds?
- Ⓐ to bury their dead
- Ⓑ for protection against severe weather
- Ⓒ to protect themselves from enemies
- Ⓓ to live in

6. In what kinds of houses did the Hopewell live?
- Ⓔ huts
- Ⓕ longhouses
- Ⓖ wigwams
- Ⓗ teepees

7. What brought an end to the Inca civilization?
- Ⓐ the bubonic plague
- Ⓑ the arrival of Pizarro
- Ⓒ a civil war
- Ⓓ an earthquake

8. In what kinds of houses did the Inuit live?
- Ⓔ sod houses
- Ⓕ longhouses
- Ⓖ log cabins
- Ⓗ adobe houses

9. The Cherokee and Mohawk were also called
- Ⓐ the Algonquin.
- Ⓑ the Anastasia.
- Ⓒ the Iroquois.
- Ⓓ all of these

10. The Hohokam are also called
- Ⓔ the First Ones.
- Ⓕ the Old Ones.
- Ⓖ the Wise Ones.
- Ⓗ the Vanished Ones.

🛑 STOP

Social Studies: African Kingdoms

Directions: Read each sentence or phrase carefully. Fill in the correct answer circle.

Sample

A. The kingdom of Mali was located in

(A) **West Africa**   (C) South Africa

(B) East Africa   (D) none of these

---

1. What region in Africa did the Soninke rule?

   (A) Mali
   (B) Ghana
   (C) Egypt
   (D) Morocco

2. What river was significant in the development of the kingdom of Mali?

   (E) the Nile
   (F) the Amazon
   (G) the Niger
   (H) none of these

3. Which city was important to trade in the kingdom of Mali?

   (A) Koumbi
   (B) Jenne-jenno
   (C) Timbuktu
   (D) none of these

4. The Zagwe Dynasty is associated with

   (E) China.
   (F) Vietnam.
   (G) Ghana.
   (H) Ethiopia.

5. Who were the original rulers of Ethiopia?

   (A) the Swahili
   (B) the Axumites
   (C) the Benin
   (D) none of these

6. What body of water was significant in trade for Ethiopia?

   (E) the Pacific Ocean
   (F) The Atlantic Ocean
   (G) the Red Sea
   (H) the Indian Ocean

7. The Swahili culture is a blending of

   (A) East African and Muslim cultures.
   (B) West African and East African cultures.
   (C) East African and Indian cultures.
   (D) Christian and Muslim cultures.

8. Which of the following did many East African kingdoms trade?

   (E) silver
   (F) ivory
   (G) maize
   (H) grain

STOP

Social Studies: Renaissance

Directions: Read each sentence or phrase carefully. Fill in the correct answer circle.

> ## Sample
> **A.** What city is considered the birthplace of the Renaissance?
> (A) London   (B) Paris   (C) Copenhagen   **(D) Florence**

1. During the Renaissance writers and thinkers drew inspiration from
   (A) the Americas.
   (B) the study of alchemy.
   (C) ancient Greece and Rome.
   (D) nobles.

2. What important technique did artists master during the Renaissance?
   (E) selective coloration
   (F) perspective
   (G) realism
   (H) none of these

3. Who painted the *Mona Lisa*?
   (A) Raphael
   (B) Michelangelo
   (C) Leonardo Da Vinci
   (D) Galileo

4. Both Copernicus and Galileo believed that
   (E) the Earth moved around the sun.
   (F) the sun moved around the Earth.
   (G) the moon moved around the sun.
   (H) the Earth moved around the moon.

5. How did the printing press fuel the Renaissance?
   (A) It increased literacy.
   (B) It enabled information and ideas to spread quicker than they had previously.
   (C) Gutenberg became an important political leader of the age.
   (D) Paper was invented.

(GO)

6. If you purchased an indulgence from the church it meant that

    Ⓔ you curried favor with the priests.

    Ⓕ your sins were immediately forgiven.

    Ⓖ Martin Luther would get angry with you.

    Ⓗ you were helping to alleviate poverty.

7. The movement to break away from the Catholic Church was called

    Ⓐ excommunication.

    Ⓑ the Counter-Reformation.

    Ⓒ Lutheranism.

    Ⓓ the Reformation.

8. Who was the first European to sail around the Cape of Good Hope?

    Ⓔ Bartolomeu Dias

    Ⓕ Henry the Navigator

    Ⓖ Magellan

    Ⓗ de Gama

9. The importation and exportation of goods between Europe and the Americas is called

    Ⓐ the Amero-Euro Exchange.

    Ⓑ the Columbian Exchange.

    Ⓒ the Atlantic Slave Trade.

    Ⓓ the Treaty of Exchange.

10. The Armada was a sea battle between

    Ⓔ Spain and France.

    Ⓕ Spain and Mexico.

    Ⓖ England and France.

    Ⓗ England and Spain.

STOP

Social Studies: World War I

Directions: Read each sentence or phrase carefully. Fill in the correct answer circle.

Sample

A. Who ruled Germany at the beginning of the 20th century?

  (A) Wilhelm I   (C) Archduke Ferdinand

  (B) Wilhelm II   (D) Nicholas II

---

1. Which countries were part of the Triple Alliance?

  (A) Great Britain, the United States, and France

  (B) Italy, Germany, and Austria-Hungary

  (C) Austria-Hungry, Turkey, and Spain

  (D) Italy, France, and Spain

2. Why was there tension between the European Powers at the beginning of the 20th century?

  (E) competition for resources in Africa and Asia

  (F) the colonization of the Americas

  (G) religious conflicts between the European powers

  (H) trade treaties

3. Russia, Great Britain, and France formed the

  (A) Triple Alliance.

  (B) Trio of London.

  (C) Triple Entente.

  (D) North Atlantic Pact.

4. What was the source of tension within Austria-Hungary?

  (E) the clash of religious ideologies

  (F) poverty and discrimination

  (G) the desire of ethnic groups to form their own countries

  (H) famine

5. Whose assassination triggered the First World War?

  (A) Queen Victoria

  (B) Czar Nicholas II

  (C) Francis Ferdinand

  (D) none of these

6. On whose side did the Ottoman Empire fight in World War I?

  (E) Austria-Hungary

  (F) France

  (G) Germany

  (H) Both E and G

7. Who were the Allied Powers?

  (A) Ottoman Empire, Austria-Hungary, and Germany

  (B) Ottoman Empire, Italy, and Germany

  (C) Italy, Germany, and France

  (D) Italy, Great Britain, France, and Russia

(GO)

8. Why were the numbers of causalities so high during World War I?

Ⓔ new and deadlier weaponry

Ⓕ poor medical treatment

Ⓖ disease

Ⓗ inexperienced soldiers

9. What event changed public opinion in America regarding World War I?

Ⓐ the sinking of the Lusitania

Ⓑ the sinking of the Titanic

Ⓒ radio broadcasts from the Western Front

Ⓓ none of these

10. In what year did the United States declare war on Germany?

Ⓔ 1915

Ⓕ 1917

Ⓖ 1920

Ⓗ 1919

11. Who was president during the First World War?

Ⓐ Franklin Roosevelt

Ⓑ Theodore Roosevelt

Ⓒ Woodrow Wilson

Ⓓ Harry Truman

12. Which treaty ended World War I?

Ⓔ Treaty of Trent

Ⓕ Treaty of Versailles

Ⓖ Treaty of Gaul

Ⓗ Treaty of Verdun

13. What organization was created after World War I?

Ⓐ the United Nations

Ⓑ NATO

Ⓒ the League of Nations

Ⓓ OPEC

14. What was Germany forced to do at the end of World War I?

Ⓔ apologize

Ⓕ allow inspectors into weapons plants

Ⓖ divide into two different countries

Ⓗ pay reparations

STOP

Social Studies: World War II

Directions: Read each sentence or phrase carefully. Fill in the correct answer circle.

Sample

A. Who was the Italian fascist leader?

Ⓐ Hitler   **Ⓒ Mussolini**

Ⓑ Tito   Ⓓ Chamberlain

---

1. Fascist ideology

Ⓐ stresses individuality.

Ⓑ stresses belief in one god.

Ⓒ stresses nationality.

Ⓓ stresses aggression.

2. What gave rise to fascism in Germany in the 1930s?

Ⓔ inflation and unemployment

Ⓕ hatred

Ⓖ lack of education

Ⓗ fear of Hitler

3. What tool did the Nazi's use to spread their ideologies?

Ⓐ newspapers

Ⓑ magazines

Ⓒ propaganda

Ⓓ television

4. To annex a country means to

Ⓔ conquer it.

Ⓕ attach it to an already existing country.

Ⓖ destroy it.

Ⓗ make the citizens all speak one language.

5. What is appeasement?

Ⓐ a policy which gives in to the demands of an aggressor to avoid conflict

Ⓑ a policy which denies the demands of an aggressor

Ⓒ a policy of annexation

Ⓓ Hitler's war strategy

6. What was the Battle of Britain?

Ⓔ a sea battle

Ⓕ a land battle

Ⓖ a battle for the Channel Islands

Ⓗ an air battle

7. What did Hitler and Stalin secretly agree to do?

Ⓐ invade Poland

Ⓑ invade Russia

Ⓒ invade Italy

Ⓓ all of these

8. Who were the Axis Powers?

Ⓔ Germany, Japan, and Italy

Ⓕ the United States, Great Britain, and the Soviet Union

Ⓖ the United States, Germany, and Spain

Ⓗ Germany, Italy, and the Soviet Union

GO

9. What is the significance of December 7th, 1941?

Ⓐ It is the date that Germany invaded Poland.

Ⓑ It is the date that the Japanese attacked Pearl Harbor.

Ⓒ It is the date of the Battle of Britain.

Ⓓ It is the date that Japan surrendered.

10. What points of commonality did Japan and Germany share?

Ⓔ They were both trying to conquer other countries.

Ⓕ They were both enemies of Poland.

Ⓖ They were both allies of Poland.

Ⓗ none of these

11. Who were the Big Three?

Ⓐ Stalin, Chamberlain, and Churchill

Ⓑ Roosevelt, Chamberlain, and Hirohito

Ⓒ Mussolini, Chamberlain, and Churchill

Ⓓ Roosevelt, Churchill, and Stalin

12. What happened on D-Day?

Ⓔ the invasion of Austria

Ⓕ the invasion of Normandy

Ⓖ the invasion of Russia

Ⓗ the attack on Pearl Harbor

13. What was the Final Solution?

Ⓐ the German conquest of Europe and Africa

Ⓑ the German conquest of China

Ⓒ the German plan to exterminate Jewish people in Europe

Ⓓ the end of World War II

14. About how many Jews were killed during World War II?

Ⓔ 1 million

Ⓕ 6 million

Ⓖ 2 million

Ⓗ no one knows for sure

15. On which two cities did the United States drop atomic bombs?

Ⓐ Berlin and Rome

Ⓑ Hiroshima and Nagasaki

Ⓒ London and Paris

Ⓓ none of these

16. What was the goal of The Marshall Plan?

Ⓔ to divide Germany

Ⓕ to create the United Nations

Ⓖ to rebuild Europe

Ⓗ none of these

STOP

Social Studies: The Cold War

Directions: Read each sentence or phrase carefully. Fill in the correct answer circle.

Sample

A. To what does the Cold War refer?

   Ⓐ the Vietnam era   Ⓒ hostile Soviets

   Ⓑ the current era   Ⓓ **the tension that existed between the Soviet Union and the United States**

---

1. What was the *iron curtain*?

   Ⓐ a kind of imaginary line that separated Communist and democratic countries in Europe

   Ⓑ the border between North and South Korea

   Ⓒ the border between North and South Vietnam

   Ⓓ the western border of Russia

---

2. The containment policy sought to

   Ⓔ send supplies to the people of Berlin.

   Ⓕ avert a crises in Cuba.

   Ⓖ limit the spread of communism.

   Ⓗ do none of these.

---

3. For what does NATO stand?

   Ⓐ Northern Alliance Treaty Organization

   Ⓑ North Atlantic Treaty Organization

   Ⓒ North Africa Treaty Organization

   Ⓓ none of these

---

4. What was NATO's mission?

   Ⓔ to attack communist countries

   Ⓕ to aid each other if attacked by the Soviets

   Ⓖ to reunify Germany

   Ⓗ none of these

---

5. In what decade was the Berlin Wall constructed?

   Ⓐ the 1960s

   Ⓑ the 1950s

   Ⓒ the 1970s

   Ⓓ the 1940s

GO

Social Studies: The Cold War *(cont.)*

6. What precipitated the Cuban Missile crisis?
- Ⓔ the construction of he Berlin wall
- Ⓕ the construction of the iron curtain
- Ⓖ the construction of missile bases in Cuba
- Ⓗ the sale of nuclear weapons to Cuba

7. To what does the Cultural Revolution refer?
- Ⓐ ridding China of counter-revolutionary elements
- Ⓑ the emergence of great art in China
- Ⓒ the building of the Red Army
- Ⓓ none of these

8. Why did the United States enter the Korean war?
- Ⓔ to help China
- Ⓕ to help Japan
- Ⓖ to help South Korea
- Ⓗ none of these

9. Who were the Viet Cong?
- Ⓐ people from south Vietnam
- Ⓑ North Vietnamese guerilla fighters
- Ⓒ South Vietnamese guerilla fighters
- Ⓓ refugees from South Vietnam

10. What was the significance of the Tet Offensive?
- Ⓔ It ended the Vietnam War.
- Ⓕ It began the Vietnam War.
- Ⓖ It caused a civil war in Cambodia.
- Ⓗ It showed American forces in Vietnam that the Viet Cong were a formidable enemy.

(STOP)

Student Answer Sheets

Page Number _____

1. Ⓐ Ⓑ Ⓒ Ⓓ
2. Ⓔ Ⓕ Ⓖ Ⓗ
3. Ⓐ Ⓑ Ⓒ Ⓓ
4. Ⓔ Ⓕ Ⓖ Ⓗ
5. Ⓐ Ⓑ Ⓒ Ⓓ
6. Ⓔ Ⓕ Ⓖ Ⓗ
7. Ⓐ Ⓑ Ⓒ Ⓓ
8. Ⓔ Ⓕ Ⓖ Ⓗ
9. Ⓐ Ⓑ Ⓒ Ⓓ
10. Ⓔ Ⓕ Ⓖ Ⓗ
11. Ⓐ Ⓑ Ⓒ Ⓓ
12. Ⓔ Ⓕ Ⓖ Ⓗ
13. Ⓐ Ⓑ Ⓒ Ⓓ
14. Ⓔ Ⓕ Ⓖ Ⓗ
15. Ⓐ Ⓑ Ⓒ Ⓓ
16. Ⓔ Ⓕ Ⓖ Ⓗ
17. Ⓐ Ⓑ Ⓒ Ⓓ
18. Ⓔ Ⓕ Ⓖ Ⓗ
19. Ⓐ Ⓑ Ⓒ Ⓓ
20. Ⓔ Ⓕ Ⓖ Ⓗ
21. Ⓐ Ⓑ Ⓒ Ⓓ
22. Ⓔ Ⓕ Ⓖ Ⓗ
23. Ⓐ Ⓑ Ⓒ Ⓓ
24. Ⓔ Ⓕ Ⓖ Ⓗ
25. Ⓐ Ⓑ Ⓒ Ⓓ

Page Number _____

1. Ⓐ Ⓑ Ⓒ Ⓓ
2. Ⓔ Ⓕ Ⓖ Ⓗ
3. Ⓐ Ⓑ Ⓒ Ⓓ
4. Ⓔ Ⓕ Ⓖ Ⓗ
5. Ⓐ Ⓑ Ⓒ Ⓓ
6. Ⓔ Ⓕ Ⓖ Ⓗ
7. Ⓐ Ⓑ Ⓒ Ⓓ
8. Ⓔ Ⓕ Ⓖ Ⓗ
9. Ⓐ Ⓑ Ⓒ Ⓓ
10. Ⓔ Ⓕ Ⓖ Ⓗ
11. Ⓐ Ⓑ Ⓒ Ⓓ
12. Ⓔ Ⓕ Ⓖ Ⓗ
13. Ⓐ Ⓑ Ⓒ Ⓓ
14. Ⓔ Ⓕ Ⓖ Ⓗ
15. Ⓐ Ⓑ Ⓒ Ⓓ
16. Ⓔ Ⓕ Ⓖ Ⓗ
17. Ⓐ Ⓑ Ⓒ Ⓓ
18. Ⓔ Ⓕ Ⓖ Ⓗ
19. Ⓐ Ⓑ Ⓒ Ⓓ
20. Ⓔ Ⓕ Ⓖ Ⓗ
21. Ⓐ Ⓑ Ⓒ Ⓓ
22. Ⓔ Ⓕ Ⓖ Ⓗ
23. Ⓐ Ⓑ Ⓒ Ⓓ
24. Ⓔ Ⓕ Ⓖ Ⓗ
25. Ⓐ Ⓑ Ⓒ Ⓓ

Answer Key

Pages 14–15—Multiple-Choice Practice Questions

1. B
2. G
3. E
4. G
5. D
6. F
7. B
8. G

Page 20—Reading Comprehension: Mercury and the Woodman

1. B literal
2. G literal

Pages 22–23—Reading Comprehension: The Pied Piper

1. B
2. G
3. D
4. E
5. B
6. F
7. D
8. F

Pages 24–25—Reading Comprehension: Nonfiction Passage

1. D
2. H
3. A
4. E
5. B
6. G
7. B
8. G

Pages 26–27—Language Arts: Complete Sentences

1. C
2. F
3. A
4. G
5. D
6. E
7. B
8. E
9. D
10. G

Page 28—Language Arts: Types of Sentences

1. B
2. E
3. D
4. F
5. D
6. E
7. C
8. E
9. B
10. H

Pages 29–30—Language Arts: Subjects and Predicates

1. B
2. H
3. B
4. G
5. D
6. G
7. B
8. E
9. D
10. F

Page 31—Language Arts: Independent and Dependent Clauses

1. A
2. C
3. B
4. C
5. A
6. D
7. B
8. C
9. B
10. C

Page 32—Language Arts: Compound and Complex Sentences

1. A
2. D
3. B
4. D
5. A
6. C
7. A
8. C
9. A
10. D

Pages 33–34—Language Arts: Sentence Combining

1. B
2. D
3. C
4. D
5. C
6. F
7. B
8. D
9. H

Answer Key (cont.)

Page 35—Language Arts: Plural Nouns
1. A
2. G
3. A
4. G
5. B
6. H
7. A
8. H

Page 36—Language Arts: Possessive Nouns
1. B
2. D
3. C
4. D
5. C
6. D
7. B
8. F
9. A
10. F

Page 37—Language Arts: Sentence Punctuation
1. C
2. E
3. C
4. D
5. C
6. F
7. A
8. F

Page 38—Language Arts: Action and Linking Verbs
1. B
2. F
3. C
4. F
5. B
6. D
7. B
8. F
9. C
10. E

Page 39—Language Arts: Verb Tense
1. A
2. F
3. B
4. D
5. C
6. E
7. A
8. D
9. C
10. E

Page 40—Language Arts: Verb Tense II
1. B
2. F
3. A
4. E
5. B
6. D
7. B
8. D
9. A
10. D

Page 41—Language Arts: Vocabulary
1. D
2. F
3. D
4. E
5. B
6. G
7. D
8. E
9. D
10. G

Page 42—Language Arts: Direct and Indirect Objects
1. B
2. F
3. C
4. E
5. A
6. H
7. A
8. F
9. C
10. H

Page 43—Language Arts: Subject Complements
1. B
2. H
3. C
4. E
5. C
6. E
7. A
8. H
9. A
10. F

Page 44—Language Arts: Adjectives
1. B
2. D
3. A
4. D
5. B
6. D
7. A
8. C
9. B
10. D
11. A
12. C

Answer Key (cont.)

Page 45—Language Arts: Adverbs

1. D
2. F
3. A
4. H
5. D
6. E
7. A
8. H
9. D
10. H

Page 46—Language Arts: Pronouns

1. A
2. F
3. A
4. F
5. D
6. H
7. A
8. F
9. C
10. H

Pages 47–48—Language Arts: Pronoun Referents

1. C
2. E
3. D
4. G
5. A
6. F
7. A
8. F
9. A
10. H

Pages 49–50—Language Arts: Prepositional Phrases

1. D
2. H

3. A
4. F
5. C
6. E
7. D
8. F
9. C
10. E

Page 51—Language Arts: Contractions

1. C
2. E
3. C
4. F
5. D
6. G
7. A
8. G

Page 52—Language Arts: Mixed Practice

1. B
2. G
3. D
4. F
5. C
6. E
7. C
8. H

Pages 53–54—Language Arts: Reading Comprehension – Food in Ancient Egypt

1. C
2. G
3. B
4. H
5. C
6. G
7. A
8. H

Pages 55–56—Language Arts: Reading Comprehension – Jabberwocky and The 6th Grade Nickname Game

1. B
2. F
3. C
4. H
5. B
6. F
7. B
8. H

Pages 57–60—Language Arts: Reading Comprehension – How the Mentally Ill Were Treated and The Iceman

1. B
2. F
3. C
4. H
5. D
6. F
7. C
8. H
9. A
10. G
11. C
12. F

Pages 63–64—Mathematics: Decimal Forms

1. C
2. F
3. A
4. F
5. A
6. H
7. A
8. E
9. C
10. E

Page 65—Mathematics:
Rounding Decimals

1. A
2. G
3. C
4. G
5. A
6. H
7. C
8. H

Pages 66–67—Mathematics:
Comparing and Ordering
Decimals and Scientific
Notation

1. A
2. G
3. A
4. G
5. A
6. G
7. A
8. H

Page 68—Mathematics:
Addition and Subtraction of
Decimals

1. B
2. G
3. A
4. F
5. D
6. G
7. C
8. E

Page 69—Mathematics:
Multiplying Decimals

1. A
2. H
3. A
4. F
5. D

6. G
7. B
8. H

Page 70—Mathematics:
Dividing Decimals

1. C
2. E
3. A
4. F
5. B
6. H
7. D
8. E

Page 71—Mathematics:
Divisibility

1. A
2. E
3. C
4. H
5. B
6. E
7. D
8. H

Page 72—Mathematics: Prime
and Composite Numbers and
Prime Factorization

1. A
2. G
3. C
4. F
5. B
6. G
7. A
8. H

Page 73—Mathematics:
Least Common Multiples and
Greatest Common Factors

1. C
2. F
3. D

4. H
5. C
6. E
7. A
8. G

Page 74—Mathematics:
Fraction Concepts

1. C
2. H
3. B
4. H
5. D
6. F
7. B
8. E

Page 75—Mathematics:
Fraction Concepts II

1. B
2. G
3. B
4. H
5. A
6. F
7. C
8. F

Page 76—Mathematics:
Converting Fractions and
Decimals

1. B
2. E
3. B
4. F
5. A
6. D
7. C
8. E
9. B
10. E

Answer Key (cont.)

Pages 77–78—Mathematics: Comparing and Ordering Fractions and Decimals

1. A
2. E
3. C
4. F
5. B
6. F
7. A
8. E
9. C
10. D
11. B
12. F

Page 79—Mathematics: Adding and Subtracting Fractions

1. B
2. H
3. B
4. H
5. C
6. F
7. A
8. H

Page 80—Mathematics: Multiplying Fractions

1. C
2. H
3. A
4. H
5. B
6. E
7. D
8. H

Page 81—Mathematics: Dividing Fractions

1. B
2. G

3. C
4. F
5. A
6. H
7. B
8. H

Page 82—Mathematics: Adding Integers

1. A
2. F
3. D
4. G
5. B
6. H
7. A
8. H

Page 83—Mathematics: Subtracting Integers

1. A
2. G
3. B
4. F
5. C
6. E
7. D
8. F

Page 84—Mathematics: Multiplying Integers

1. A
2. G
3. C
4. H
5. B
6. F
7. D
8. E

Page 85—Mathematics: Dividing Integers

1. B

2. G
3. A
4. F
5. C
6. E
7. D
8. E

Page 86—Mathematics: The Coordinate Plane

1. A
2. F
3. C
4. H
5. B
6. G
7. D
8. E
9. B
10. F

Page 87—Mathematics: Ratio and Rate

1. A
2. G
3. B
4. H
5. C
6. F
7. B
8. H

Page 88—Mathematics: Proportions

1. B
2. H
3. C
4. G
5. A
6. H
7. D
8. E

Page 89—Mathematics: Geometry

1. B
2. F
3. D
4. G
5. D
6. E
7. C
8. H
9. B
10. F

Page 90—Mathematics: Percents, Decimals, and Fractions

1. B
2. F
3. B
4. E
5. D
6. G
7. A
8. E
9. D
10. F

Page 91—Science: Weather I

1. A
2. F
3. D
4. G
5. D
6. F
7. A
8. E
9. D
10. F

Page 92—Science: Weather II

1. B
2. E
3. A
4. E
5. B
6. H
7. C
8. E
9. A
10. G

Page 93—Science: Geology I

1. D
2. G
3. B
4. E
5. C
6. E
7. A
8. G
9. B
10. H

Page 94—Science: Geology II

1. B
2. G
3. A
4. H
5. B
6. G
7. D
8. H
9. A
10. H

Page 95—Science: Astronomy I

1. B
2. G
3. A
4. H
5. B
6. E
7. B

8. H
9. C
10. H

Page 96—Science: Astronomy II

1. D
2. F
3. D
4. G
5. A
6. G
7. D
8. E
9. C
10. F

Page 97—Science: Astronomy III

1. C
2. F
3. A
4. G
5. B
6. G
7. A
8. G
9. B
10. G

Page 98—Science: Biology I

1. B
2. G
3. D
4. F
5. C
6. E
7. A
8. F
9. C
10. E

Answer Key (cont.)

Page 99—Science: Biology II

1. B
2. H
3. B
4. E
5. C
6. F
7. A
8. H
9. A
10. G

Page 100—Science: Biology III

1. C
2. G
3. A
4. G
5. D
6. F
7. C
8. H
9. B
10. F

Page 101—Science: Biology IV

1. B
2. E
3. B
4. F
5. C
6. G
7. A
8. H
9. D
10. H

Pages 102–103—Science: Environment

1. C
2. G
3. B
4. F

5. C
6. F
7. C
8. H
9. D
10. E
11. C
12. E
13. C
14. F
15. D

Pages 104–105—Science: Light and Sound

1. D
2. F
3. B
4. E
5. D
6. G
7. C
8. H
9. B
10. E
11. B
12. G
13. A
14. F
15. B

Page 106—Science: Heat

1. C
2. F
3. A
4. F
5. C
6. F
7. C
8. G
9. D
10. H

Page 107—Science: Chemistry

1. C
2. F
3. D
4. F
5. D
6. G
7. D
8. H
9. B
10. F
11. A
12. G
13. A
14. H
15. B
16. G

Pages 109–110—Science: Force and Motion

1. D
2. G
3. C
4. F
5. A
6. H
7. D
8. G
9. D
10. E
11. C
12. E
13. D
14. E
15. B

Pages 111–112—Science: Health and Human Body

1. C
2. E
3. D

4. F
5. C
6. F
7. C
8. E
9. C
10. E
11. D
12. H
13. D
14. H
15. C

Pages 113–114—Social Studies: Pre-History

1. B
2. H
3. B
4. E
5. D
6. G
7. A
8. H
9. B
10. F
11. A
12. H
13. A
14. G
15. A

Page 115—Social Studies: Early Civilizations

1. B
2. G
3. D
4. E
5. C
6. E
7. C
8. H

9. B
10. E

Pages 116–117—Social Studies: Ancient Civilizations

1. D
2. G
3. A
4. G
5. B
6. E
7. A
8. G
9. C
10. E
11. D
12. F
13. A
14. H
15. B
16. G
17. B
18. E
19. C
20. E

Pages 118–119—Social Studies: Ancient Greece

1. C
2. G
3. D
4. G
5. C
6. E
7. C
8. F
9. D
10. G
11. A
12. H
13. C

Pages 120–121—Social Studies: Ancient Rome

1. A
2. G
3. B
4. G
5. B
6. E
7. C
8. G
9. B
10. G
11. B
12. G
13. D

Pages 122–123—Social Studies: The Middle Ages

1. C
2. H
3. A
4. E
5. A
6. C
7. H
8. C
9. E
10. H
11. G
12. E
13. B

Page 124—Social Studies: Mesoamerica

1. A
2. H
3. C
4. H
5. D
6. E
7. C

8. F

9. C

10. H

Page 125—Social Studies: Native People of North and South America

1. C

2. E

3. D

4. F

5. A

6. G

7. B

8. E

9. C

10. H

Page 126—Social Studies: African Kingdoms

1. B

2. G

3. C

4. H

5. B

6. F

7. C

8. E

Pages 127–128—Social Studies: Renaissance

1. C

2. F

3. C

4. E

5. B

6. F

7. D

8. E

9. B

10. H

Pages 129–130—Social Studies: World War I

1. B

2. E

3. C

4. G

5. C

6. H

7. D

8. E

9. A

10. F

11. C

12. F

13. C

14. H

Pages 131–132—Social Studies: World War II

1. C

2. E

3. C

4. F

5. A

6. H

7. A

8. E

9. B

10. E

11. D

12. F

13. C

14. F

15. B

16. G

Pages 133–134—Social Studies: The Cold War

1. A

2. G

3. B

4. F

5. A

6. G

7. A

8. G

9. B

10. H